William Harold Payne, Gabriel Compayré

The elements of psychology

William Harold Payne, Gabriel Compayré

The elements of psychology

ISBN/EAN: 9783337277918

Printed in Europe, USA, Canada, Australia, Japan

Cover: Foto ©Thomas Meinert / pixelio.de

More available books at **www.hansebooks.com**

THE

ELEMENTS OF PSYCHOLOGY

BY

GABRIEL COMPAYRÉ

GRADUATE OF THE ÉCOLE NORMAL SUPÉRIEURE, FELLOW IN
PHILOSOPHY, DOCTOR OF LETTERS, PROFESSOR
IN THE UNIVERSITY

TRANSLATED BY

WILLIAM H. PAYNE, Ph.D., LL.D.

CHANCELLOR OF THE UNIVERSITY OF NASHVILLE, AND PRESIDENT OF THE
PEABODY NORMAL COLLEGE; AUTHOR OF "CHAPTERS ON SCHOOL
SUPERVISION," "OUTLINES OF EDUCATIONAL DOCTRINE,"
AND "CONTRIBUTIONS TO THE SCIENCE OF EDU-
CATION"; TRANSLATOR OF COMPAYRÉ'S
"HISTOIRE DE PÉDAGOGIE" AND
"COURS DE PÉDAGOGIE"

BOSTON
LEE AND SHEPARD PUBLISHERS
10 MILK STREET
1895

Paris, June 13, 1890.

Prof. W. H. PAYNE.

Dear Sir:— Full authorization is granted you for the translation of my *Psychologie.* I thank you for thus adding my *Notions Élémentaires de Psychologie* to your beautiful translations of my *Histoire de la Pédagogie* and my *Leçons de Pédagogie.*

. . . .

Yours, under great obligations,

GABRIEL COMPAYRÉ.

THE ELEMENTS OF PSYCHOLOGY.

TRANSLATOR'S PREFACE.

THOUGH many works on Psychology have been pub.
lished within the last few years, the feeling is still very
general that even the best of them are not well adapted
to the needs of teachers who are in quest of principles
and doctrines which may serve as a basis for rational
methods. It is to be recollected that neither the highest generalizations nor the mere empirical rules of a
science can be turned to profitable account in the way
of practical applications ; the first are too vague to
admit of ready interpretation and use ; and the second
are too narrow to be fruitful in adaptations to an art
where versatility is so necessary. A book to serve the
needs of the general teaching class should have, it
would seem, the following qualities : —

1. It should contain only the essentials of psychol
ogy ; it should not be a cyclopædia of psychological
science.

2. It should not be a work of erudition or learned
research, designed for the specialist and the proficient ;
but a book for the dissemination of scientific truth
among persons who need it first of all for the applications they can make of it.

3. It should be written in terms readily intelligible by ordinary readers; it should not require any extraordinary scientific acumen or power of interpretation.

4. As most teachers of youth are believers in the spirituality of the soul, and in the absolute dissimilarity of mind and matter, they prefer a book whose tone and treatment are in accord with the Christian spirit.

It is because Compayré's *Notions Élémentaires de Psychologie* seems to embody these qualities to a greater degree than any other book with which I am acquainted, that I have undertaken its translation.

Those who are acquainted with M. Compayré's excellences as a thinker and a writer will need no assurance that his *Psychologie* is characterized by philosophic insight, wisdom in the selection of matter, accuracy of views, and absolute clearness in exposition.

M. Compayré's experience as an instructor in normal schools has enabled him to determine the kind and amount of matter, mode of exposition, and sequence of topics, which are best adapted to the intellectual and professional needs of the teaching class.

One charm of the book lies in the fact that Psychology, under this mode of treatment, has all the concrete interest of physical science. The subject is no longer enveloped in transcendental obscurity, but is brought within the compass of the ordinary intelligence by being presented as an experimental science, or science of observation.

M. Compayré's philosophy will be congenial to English readers, for it is the philosophy of common-sense. "Spontaneity, impersonality, and universality," says M. Jaques, "are the characteristics of truths of *common-sense;* and hence their truth and certainty. The moral law, human liberty, the existence of God, and immortality of the soul, are truths of *common-sense.*"

My immediate purpose in making this translation has been to provide a suitable book for the large classes of professional students in the Peabody Normal College; but my thought beyond this has been to provide the thousands of readers of Compayré's History and Lectures with a companion volume and sequel.

W. H. PAYNE.

University of Nashville,
    Peabody Normal College,
        May 14, 1890.

CONTENTS.

INTRODUCTION

REASONS FOR TEACHING PSYCHOLOGY, AND THE METHOD BY WHICH IT SHOULD BE TAUGHT

1. Object of this Introduction. — Before entering upon the subject proper two preliminary questions ought to be settled : —

1. Why has the study of Psychology, hitherto reserved by way of privilege to collegiate instruction of the classical type, been recently introduced into our primary instruction, and into the programme of our normal schools, just as, still more recently, it has been included to a certain extent in the course of study for special schools ?

2. How shall Psychology be taught, and what are the best methods to be employed for acclimating this philosophical science on this new territory, in order that it may produce all its results in minds apparently ill prepared for this class of studies ?

2. General Utility of Psychology. — Though the progress of thought has transformed human knowledge and has created new sciences of marvellous scope, we are still justified in repeating, after the lapse of two thousand years, what Socrates attempted to teach each of his disciples : the first and the most useful of the sciences is that which is summed up in this simple maxim, " Know thyself."

In fact, the knowledge of one's self is the key to all the moral sciences. To know one's self is at the same time to know all men ; it is to grasp the principles upon which rest all the knowledges relative to the moral nature of humanity.

History would be but an incoherent succession of facts, an enigmatic procession of characters whose parts are not understood, for one who has not learned, in the school of psychology, to disentangle the inner motives, ideas, sentiments, or passions which move humanity, — for one who cannot analyze the characters of the men who, by their preponderant action, are the principal makers of history.

So also, without a knowledge of men, one would never be more than a mediocre statesman ; for, to govern men, the first condition is to know what are the essential instincts, the natural aspirations of humanity. How can we assume to direct forces whose nature is unknown to us ?

3. Psychology and Morals. — But the utility of psychology is made manifest still more strikingly in its relations to ethics and pedagogy.

Theoretically, ethics is based on psychology. Liberty, which conditions the existence of morals, and con-

science, which is its governing law, — liberty and conscience are psychological facts. The principles of
ethics are really intelligible only to those who have
traced their origin to psychology and have tested their
validity in their own consciousness. On the other
hand, the theory of duty is nothing but an induction,
an inference from psychological facts. It is what we
are that teaches us to determine what we ought to be.
It is the knowledge of his own nature that reveals to
man his destiny. For the most part, duties are but
natural tendencies moderated and governed by the
reason.

Practically, ethics has no less need of psychology.
How many faults we might have shunned, how many
virtues we might have acquired, had we been able to
reflect as psychologists on the efficacy of an effort of a
courageous will, on the omnipotence of habit, on the
inevitable fatality of a passion which is not controlled
by reflection and repressed by the will!

4. Psychology and Pedagogy. — What shall we say of
the influence exercised by a well-constructed system
of psychology on pedagogy, or the science and art of
education? [1]

With respect to moral education, it is evident that
we shall make a clumsy use of the means of discipline,
that we shall be unskilful in correcting the faults and

[1] On the relations between pedagogy and psychology consult Compayré's
Lectures on Pedagogy, Chapter I.

in developing the virtues of our pupils, if psychology
does not enable us to analyze the feelings and the
passions of the child, their origin and their progress.
How shall we handle punishments and rewards with
tact, if we do not take account of the emotions which
they excite in the heart of the pupil, if we do not know
what fear and shame, what self-love and emulation are?
How shall we be successful in promoting the development and progress of moral qualities, if we have not
reflected on the relations between feelings and ideas,
and on the formation of habits?

If it is a question of intellectual education, the necessity of psychological knowledge is made still more
manifest.   What more efficient preparation could we
devise for a future educator of the mind than a study
of the mind itself, of the different faculties of which it
is composed and of the laws which govern its organization and determine the relation of its parts? And
when it becomes necessary to select the best methods
of teaching, to adapt them to the powers of the child,
and to bring them into conformity with the progress of
his intelligence, is it enough simply to have a good
knowledge of what we teach, say of history or geometry? Is it not indispensable, in order that the matter
taught may be thoroughly appropriated, to know the
working of the intellectual faculties, just as the farmer
is not satisfied when he has selected his seed, but must
also know the nature of the soil on which he sows it?

5. Psychology and Primary Instruction. — These considerations are amply sufficient to justify the introduction of psychology into the course of study for normal schools. No doubt this is knowledge which the pupil-teacher will have no occasion to communicate directly to his future pupils. It is not proposed to introduce the study of the human mind into the primary schools, notwithstanding the opinion of certain Spanish teachers who believe they can initiate their pupils into the elements of psychology, without difficulty and even with success, at the earliest period of their school life ; [1] and also notwithstanding the declaration of our French educator, Condillac, who considered the study of psychology as the instrument best adapted to illumine the mind of the child at the beginning of his studies. No ; psychology presupposes a maturity of mind and a power of attention of which the child is incapable.

But these conditions no longer affect the pupil-teacher, who is already an adolescent, accustomed to intellectual toil ; he is surely in a condition to acquire psychological knowledge without special difficulty, and, once acquired, this knowledge will be to him of inestimable value :

1. *For his Professional Education.* — As a teacher, he will be required to give instruction in morals. How can he do this satisfactorily if psychological reflection

[1] We allude to the programme now followed by the professors of the Free Academy of Madrid.

has not prepared him to comprehend the delicate and profound ideas which underlie a course in ethics, and to assimilate, by a personal effort, the abstract maxims with which he attempts to indoctrinate the mind and heart of his pupils ?

On the other hand, for the other parts of his work, as in civics and especially in history, psychology will afford him general insight and illumination which will vivify and elevate his instruction.

We hear it said over and over again that the mission of teachers is to make men. How can they do this if they are ignorant of what human nature is ?

2. *For his General Education.* — The normal school is not simply a manufactory of teachers; it owes to its pupils, in addition to the professional education which fits them for their future vocation, the general education which develops and exalts their faculties. From this point of view, psychological studies are also of the highest importance. They alone reveal to us the dignity of human nature ; they alone assign to man his proper rank, neither too high nor too low, by giving him a clear comprehension of what he is.

6. **Method of Teaching Psychology.** — But, that the pupil may actually derive these advantages from the study of psychology, the thing which is important above everything else is the manner in which this science is to be taught.

Let us note in the first place that we too often forget

the difference which exists between the scientific study of psychology, and elementary study in psychology. Psychology properly so called, psychology considered as a science, the object of profound philosophic research, is one thing; while the psychology for school use, the psychology that is taught, is quite another. This distinction has long been observed in the case of sciences that are even more readily acquired, as history, for example. We are in no danger of confounding an historian, and a professor of history; a book of scholarly erudition like Henri Martin's *Histoire de France*, and books for school use like the manuals which are in the hands of pupils. The authors of treatises on psychology are not always inspired by the same wisdom. Their works are monuments erected in behalf of science, rather than books for popular use and general education.

The teacher of psychology will then recollect, at the very start, that in the science which he teaches there is a choice to be made between discussions that are merely scholarly or knotty, useless facts, trifling details, and really useful questions which are of practical interest and which, at the same time, by their simplicity and clearness, are within easy comprehension of younger minds. Even these questions he will not profess to fathom or to exhaust; he will not discuss them as a scholar who ventures to the very limits of his researches, but he will make them as light as possible to his pupils,

and will grasp only their substance, their essential parts.
In a word, he will recollect that he is not a thinker who
is toiling and speculating for the advancement of pure
science, but a teacher who selects, who appropriates,
who simplifies scientific notions for the instruction of
his pupils.

7. Different Aims of a Course in Psychology. — The
teaching of psychology takes different forms according
to circumstances.   It may follow different directions
according to the end which is kept in view.   If we are
to teach psychology to future statesmen, lawyers, and
embryo magistrates, it is evident that they must be
made to study chiefly the psychology of the mature
man, because in the practice of their profession they
will have to do only with grown men.   But as·it is the
purpose of the normal school to train future teachers
who will have the direction of children, their attention
must be called, not only to the adult faculties in their
regular and systematic play, in the perfect and unchange-
able forms of maturity, but particularly to the psychology of the child, to the laws which regulate the growth,
development, and progressive organization of his faculties.

Doubtless psychology is one, and in the normal school,
as well as in the college or the university, it always
admits the same questions, studied almost in the same
order.   However, by reason of the nature of his instruction, the normal-school professor must needs give pref-

erence to certain subjects, as the laws of habit, for example ; but will pass rapidly over others, such as the
origin of ideas. He will adapt the development of his
theme to the practical utility of the subjects treated.
Finally, to all the questions which he discusses, he will
give that particular treatment indicated by the special
destination of the pupils to whom he addresses himself.

8. Natural Psychology. — But, it will be said, however
delicate the discernment of the teacher in the choice of
subjects, and in the treatment of his themes, psychological notions are nevertheless obscure notions, difficult
to comprehend, and unintelligible to certain minds.
" Psychology," contemporary authorities [1] are fond of
saying, " is an abstract and austere science ; " and common opinion is in accord with this assertion.

Are not psychologists themselves somewhat at fault
if their science is encumbered with these prejudices
and with this unenviable reputation ? Have they always made sufficient effort to find, in the very experience of the child, the starting-point for their theories ?

A prudent teacher will be able to make his pupils
comprehend, at the very beginning of his instruction,
that the principles of psychological knowledge are
already within their reach. "Of all the facts of which
he speaks to his pupils, there is not one in reality which
is not already known to them, which does not come
each moment within their experience, and the expres-

1 M. Janet, *Cours de Morale*, Introduction.

sion of which they have not found an hundred times in the authors which they have read. The teaching of philosophy, then, does not begin by throwing the pupil into an unknown world ; on the contrary, it places him on his most familiar soil ; it takes for basis a science which he has already acquired, that natural psychology, common to all, which it merely aims to transform into a truly scientific psychology through exact analyses which end in precision, in classification, and in definition." [1]

Let there be a constant appeal, then, to the personal observation of the pupil, who has only to retire into himself to find there, in very fact, the phenomena whose laws his teacher is expounding. Psychological truths do not descend from the clouds of abstract thought ; they proceed, so to speak, from the very heart of man ; each one carries them within himself. There is needed, doubtless, in order to disengage them, an effort of the reflective consciousness ; but the instinctive consciousness which accompanies all the acts of the moral life is the natural starting-point for this scientific observation. "No knowledge of mental science," say American teachers, "is of any value to the teacher, which does not arise from the conscious examination and classification of the phenomena and faculties of his own mind. . . . The study of a text-book on psychology may be as purely an objective process as the examination of a

[1] M. Rabier, Discourse pronounced at the distribution of prizes, *Journal officiel*, August 4, 1886.

mineral." [1] In order, then, to make the text-book useful, and the instruction of the teacher fruitful, the pupil
must supplement them by subjective observation, and
must test them by a personal verification of the facts
stated and the laws formulated.

If this is the best means of making clear a course of
instruction in psychology, it is also the true way to
make it useful ; for it is much more important to inspire
pupils with a taste for reflection, and to give them the
habit of studying themselves, than to communicate to
them the results of a ready-made science ; just as in
morals the purpose is much rather to awaken the moral
sense and a vivid and profound consciousness of obligation,·than to teach a catalogue of duties or a series of
subtile distinctions as to good and evil.

9. Intuition in Psychology. — It follows from what
precedes, that the intuitive method will find an easy
application in the teaching of psychology. In fact, intuition assumes that children are put in the presence of
things, and that they are first shown the facts, with
which they are the most familiar. Now what is more
really present to the mind than the mind itself? What
is nearer us and more familiar to our thoughts than the
daily events of our moral life? It is wrong to represent
psychological facts as abstractions. They do not fall
under the senses, it is true ; but they are immediately
apprehended by the consciousness and gathered up by

1 See the report of the St. Cloud Normal School, for the year 1886–87.

the memory. In their way, they are real, concrete things, which the pupil may constantly place under his gaze. Memory, attention, reason, will, are facts just as truly as weight, light, and electricity are. Conceived in this spirit, with a constant appeal to the consciousness of the pupil, the lesson in psychology may become a real object lesson.

10. The Socratic Method. — The teacher of psychology will not then depend on the didactic method alone. He will not be satisfied with giving, *ex professo*, precise definitions and exact descriptions. He will interrogate his pupils as much as possible ; he will ever call into play their own powers of observation ; he will demand of them illustrations which they will find in themselves ; by directing their attention he will lead them to discover what he wishes to teach them. It is precisely to questions of the psychological order that Socrates applied the method that bears his name. When history is taught, the teacher, so to speak, is the only one who talks ; he has nothing, or almost nothing, to expect from the co-operation of his pupils ; he discovers to them facts of which they previously had no idea. When he teaches psychology, on the contrary, he may, if he knows how to go about it, have his pupils for active co-adjutors ; he may make them discover for themselves, for example, the conditions of attention, the principal laws of memory, the advantages and disadvantages of the imagination. The consciousness and the memory are for each one of us an inner museum where the different facts which constitute the object of psychological research have been successively accumulated since our infancy, since our entrance into conscious life. The task of the teachers of psychology is merely to classify these facts, to define them, and finally to introduce a scientific order into this confused and disordered collection of inner recollections.

11. **Inward Observation and the Observation of other Men.** — Just as inward observation is the basis of scientific researches into human nature, so it ought to remain the principal instrument for the teaching of psychology. Of all the sciences, psychology is the one which is best adapted to be taught by the same method by which it was discovered, — by a perpetual return of man upon himself. But it is also proper not to neglect the other sources whence may be drawn a more complete knowledge of human nature. The teacher of psychology, while inviting the pupil to observe himself, will also lead him to observe his comrades and men in general. If it is not really possible to penetrate directly into the consciousness of his fellows, he may at least divine their thoughts and emotions through gestures and signs, — the language, in a word, which expresses them.

12. **Psychology and the other Sciences.** — Psychologists generally make great efforts to prove that theirs is a distinct science, that it has its own proper object irre-

ducible to any other. We do not deny this; but in the teaching of psychology it would be very dangerous, under pretext of specializing this study, to isolate it from all others and to neglect to profit by the aid that is offered it by other sciences which, after having contributed towards establishing it, may contribute still more towards simplifying and vivifying the teaching of it. Of this number are language, history, and literature.

13. Psychology and Grammar.— It is so far from being true that psychology is a science so entirely distinct from others, and of a nature to disconcert pupils by its absolute novelty, that, on the contrary, it has intimate relations with the first science which the child undertakes, namely, grammar. A good knowledge of grammar is an excellent preparation for an important part of the course in psychology. Psychology, as we know, studies the laws of thought, and grammar, the laws of language. Now language is but the expression of thought. How then can we take account of the value of words, of their relations, of the rules of syntax which determine their correct use, without at the same time acquiring some idea of the inner processes of thought? We are studying psychology without knowing it when we make a logical analysis of the sentence, — when we distinguish the subject, the verb and predicate, which are precisely the elements of the judgment. When we state the grammatical theory of the substantive and the adjective, we apply, without suspecting it, one of the rational principles determined by psychology, namely, the principle of substance, which is sometimes enunciated as follows: "There is no quality or mode without substance."

14. Psychology and History.—Complaint is made, and not without reason, of the barrenness of a mere psychological statement which is limited to generalities on human nature. An excellent remedy for this tedious dryness felt by young minds, is to find in historical events and in the biography of illustrious men, examples corresponding to the different faculties which are studied. It is not merely to supply the defects of individual observation, which never presents to us more than an imperfect specimen of man, that we must put history under contribution; but chiefly that we may cause instruction to be penetrated with interest and life. Make your pupils perceive that in history, Newton represents attention; Cæsar, ambition; Shakespeare, imagination; Descartes, reason, and they will listen to you with redoubled curiosity. Make them comprehend what motives Charles IX. obeyed when he ordered the massacre of St. Bartholomew; Charlotte Corday, when she killed Marat; and you will have done much to initiate and interest your auditors in the study of the sensibilities. History, so to speak, is nothing but psychology in action. Historical events are to psychology nearly what experiments are to physics. They show us the human faculties acting under particular circumstances, with the relief and scope given them in the case of certain men by exceptional force of mind and character.

15. Psychology and Literature. — We also recommend that the teacher unite psychology and literature as closely as possible. The writings of moralists, the memoirs of literary men, and the works of dramatic poets are psychological documents of incomparable value. They unveil the human soul, some in the disorder of its passions, others in the heroism of its will. "For the study of the laws of the understanding, we must know men of letters; while in the tragic poets we must make an intimate study of heart, passion, and will." [1] The reading of a page of Descartes to explain the process of reasoning; of a play of Racine or of Corneille, to analyze the play of the passions ; these will come as a happy relief to didactic instruction in psychology.

16. Comparative Psychology. — Psychology furnishes man with his true titles of nobility by revealing to him the dignity of his nature ; but it should also teach him in what respect he resembles other animals. For the study of the lower faculties of human nature, — instinct, physical activity, sense-perception, memory, — animal life offers points of comparison to which the teacher of

[1] M. Janet, *La Psychologie de Racine*, Revue des Deux-Mondes, September 15, 1875.

psychology will not fail to have recourse. Children and youth have a particular taste for the observation of lower animals. We should know how to take advantage of this disposition, inasmuch as comparative psychology — the study of the animal — will contribute towards promoting the study of man. "If there were no animals," said Buffon, "the nature of man would be much more incomprehensible." If the *Fables of La Fontaine* are often lessons in morals, a given page of natural history may be also a lesson in psychology.

17. Psychology of the Child. — The study of a child, even more than the observation of animals, will furnish the psychologist with useful and interesting information. Anecdotes borrowed from the acts and pranks of children will come in play to embellish the somewhat monotonous ground-work of psychological theory. Moreover, the psychology of the child forms an integral part of a course in psychology, if it is true, as we have said elsewhere, that psychology is not a geometry of invariable theorems, but a history which relates the progressive evolution of the soul. However, a start has been made in this direction; books on childhood are multiplying;[1] and now what we have to fear in this direction is abuse and excess, rather than negligence or oversight. We have read, not without some solicitude, the dissertation of a teacher on the development of the intelligence, in

[1] The reader will consult with profit the books so suggestive and so rich in facts, which Pérez has devoted to the study of childhood.

which he speaks for several pages of the first sensations of the child before its birth !

18. Practical Advice. — We have attempted to define the general method of teaching psychology ; but, after all, it must be remembered that the best method will never supply the place of talent and learning on the part of the teacher. The lessons most in accord with the plans which we have sketched will still amount to nothing if the teacher does not know how to animate them by exactness and vivacity of exposition, and by the accent of personal conviction. However, each lesson in psychology must provide for definitions and descriptions, or rather analyses, which are but more exact descriptions. Psychology does not deserve the reproach of not being able to escape vagueness and uncertainty ; this is true only of rational psychology, which raises the metaphysical questions of substance and of the spirituality of the soul. But elementary psychology, which contents itself with stating facts and defining their relations, — empirical psychology, which does not pass the limits of observation, — is a science as solid and as exact as physics or chemistry, with only this difference, that it cannot apply numerical formulæ to the phenomena which it studies. We must endeavor, therefore, to adopt a rigor of treatment which it is not impossible to attain, while shunning, as much as possible, technical terms, and taking care, every time that we employ them, to show that they have equivalents in common language, — that sensibility and understanding, for example, are called in every-day language, heart and intellect. The examples borrowed from history, and the literary comparisons, will come into play only to complete and illustrate the didactic part of the exposition, like illustrations in the text.

19. Written Reviews. — But besides paying due regard to precision and exactness of exposition, the teacher must assure himself by frequent interrogations that the pupil has comprehended and retained what has been taught him, and must be made to add to this, from his own resources, something coming from personal reflection. In order to fix the oral instruction, it will also be well to employ the process of written review ; on condition that no abuse is made of it, and that the long task of reproducing each lesson is not imposed on every pupil. It is sufficient that pupils take turns in restating the teacher's exposition. This unique recitation, in which the pupil will be able, on certain points at least, to do original work, and which will not be merely a servile and mechanical reproduction of what has been said in class, — this written review, once revised and corrected by the teacher, will become for every pupil the exact *memento* of each part of the course.

20. Use of the Text-Book. — Under these conditions, it would seem that the text-book is not useless ; and it certainly is not. Of all the sciences, philosophy perhaps is the one which can be the least content with an oral exposition, even when excellently made; it demands, in addition, the toil of meditation and of reflective reading. Hence the necessity of a book which is a commentary on the teacher's lessons, and which, having more precision and briefer developments than an oral exposition, fixes and holds under the pupil's eyes the fundamental notions of the science.

21. General Characteristics of Psychology. — When thus taught, we do not hesitate to say that psychology may be made for young people a study relatively easy and interesting. It is with this hope that we have written the modest treatise which we now offer to our readers. May they acquire by studying it the taste for psychological studies, and the sense of the moral life, which the rising generation is in danger of losing through the development of the physical sciences! We hope at least that they will learn to esteem psychology and to comprehend its scope. The moral world, like the physical world, is subject to law; so that while studying himself a man studies all men, just as by studying one mineral or one plant, he studies all minerals and all plants. Whatever may be said of it, psychology is a positive science which, on valid grounds, aspires to certitude. It reveals to us one part of the universal order, — the order which presides over the development of our moral nature. We are not prepared to believe that it loses its value and its interest because it has waived, after the example of the physical sciences, the insoluble problems with which the human reason will always come into collision, and which fall within the domain of metaphysics, — because it has reduced its pretensions to the classification and analysis of facts which serve as the bases for moral rules and educational methods.

THE ELEMENTS OF PSYCHOLOGY

NOTE. — This mark (*) refers the reader to the Special Index of Proper Names and Technical Terms, at the end of this volume.

CHAPTER I

OBJECT OF PSYCHOLOGY. DEFINITION AND CLASSIFICATION OF PSYCHOLOGICAL FACTS

22. Definition of Terms. — Psychology — (*from two Greek words signifying science of the soul*) — is a philosophical science which studies the inner facts of the moral life of man ; just as physiology is a biological science whose object is the functions of the organic life.

Psychology is thus a science of facts which, like all facts, may be called *phenomena*, that is, things which appear ; which facts are also functions or operations, if we regard them as the prolonged manifestations of one and the same force ; and which, finally, having the common characteristic of being conscious, may be called *states of consciousness*.

Consciousness is the immediate knowledge which we have of whatever takes place in any given part of our being. The facts revealed by consciousness are connected with what is called the *moral* nature of man,

or, in other terms, with the spirit or soul; the facts
which escape consciousness, and which can be known
only through the medium of the senses, constitute, on
the other hand, the *physical* nature of man, or, in other
terms, the organism, the body. Psychology thus studies the facts of which we are conscious, and establishes
the laws which regulate them. Law is the constant
relation which exists between two phenomena, one of
which is the antecedent, or cause, and the other the
consequent, or effect.

23. Empirical Psychology and Rational Psychology. —
Psychology proper, or *Empirical Psychology*, which re-
stricts itself to observation and experience, does not
speculate upon the nature of the principle underlying
the facts which it studies. Whether this principle be
the material organism, and in particular the brain, or,
on the contrary, an immaterial cause, an independent
substance, is in one sense of little importance to this
science; it studies real facts, and this suffices for it.

If psychology wishes to go farther and pronounce
upon the existence or the nature of the soul, it becomes
Rational Psychology, which is but a part of metaphysics,
that is, of that collection of researches whose object is
whatever passes beyond nature, moral nature as well
as physical nature.[1] But just as the physicist and the
physiologist refer the facts which they observe to a

---

[1] Of the eighteen chapters composing this book, the last is the only one per-
taining to rational psychology.

single principle, matter, however embarrassed they may be to tell in just what matter consists; so, psychologists, in order to designate the supposed cause of the states of consciousness, employ the word spirit or the word soul, although they do not always trust themselves to define its nature. Were it only for clearness of exposition, it would still be necessary to hold to the word "soul" as the synonyme for the body of moral facts or conscious facts, even were it to be proved that all the conditions, all the causes, of psychological facts reside in the material organism of man.

24. History of the Idea of the Soul. — The soul has been conceived under a multitude of forms. Among primitive peoples, it seems that the belief in the soul was created by the phenomena of dreaming and the manifestations of life. On the one hand, struck by seeing again in their dreams, as if they still lived and were really present, persons whom space or death had separated from them, savages were naturally led to believe in phantoms and spirits. On the other hand, the concealed power which animates the living man and which vanishes when he dies, was early taken as a distinct principle, independent of the body. The vital soul, the phantom soul, — such are the two forms conceived by the gross spiritualism of infant peoples. For them the soul is not the prerogative of man; there is a soul in the animal and even in the plant. Just as humanity began with *polytheism* * in its conception of God, so it began with *polyanimism** in its conception of the soul. The primitive races readily regarded animals as fellow-creatures of men, attributing to them immortal souls and believing in a paradise of animals. The Esquimaux, it is said, bury in the tomb of little children the head of a dog, so that the soul of the dog may serve as a guide, towards the sojourn of the happy, to the soul of the child still incapable of self-conduct.

For a long time there was a belief in the soul of plants. In the time of St. Augustine * the Manichæans * maintained this belief. Not only so, but in-animate things, such as minerals, tools, and arms, were at first thought to have souls. Among the Fijians, in Oceanica, paradise receives the souls of hatchets and shears when these instruments have been broken in the service of men.

In a word, at the beginning of human thought, the soul was considered as a universal principle inherent in all things ; in inanimate things the soul was the principle of permanence and form ; in animals and plants it was the principle of life, of sensibility, and of motion.

25. Material Souls. — But the sensible imagination of men for a long time regarded these multiple souls as material. According to the early Greek philosophers, the human soul is of the same nature as the material elements of the universe ; at one time it is confounded with the air, and at another with fire. The early theorists of the soul were particularly struck with the idea that it is a principle of motion ; so it was conceived as something winged or mobile. The butterfly is taken as the symbol of the soul, and the Greek word *Psyche* has these two meanings. Democritus * conceives the soul as a spheroidal atom, because round bodies move more easily and glide over things more readily. We also meet with this same materialistic conception of the soul in the early fathers of the Christian church. Tertullian,* Arnobius,* St. Irenæus,* and St. Justin * still believe that the soul is a body. Among the Chinese, when a man is dead a hole is made in the roof in order that the soul may escape ; and among certain savage tribes a hole is made in the grave with the same intent. Even to-day, in certain parts of Europe, the custom is still kept up of leaving a door or a window open in the chamber of the dead.

26. The Immaterial Soul. — The idea of an immaterial soul, absolutely distinct from the body, is an idea relatively new in the history of the human mind. Plato,* a Greek philosopher, St. Augustine,* a father of the Church, and Descartes,* a French philosopher, are the real founders of the doctrine of spirituality. For Plato,* the soul is in the body like a prisoner in his cell or like a pilot in his boat. "Everything which is not matter," says St. Augustine, "and which still exists, is called spirit." Finally, Descartes, with still more precision, opposed unextended and invisible thought to material extension, and hence inferred the existence of a spiritual soul.

But Descartes, while attempting to make more clear the difference between the soul and the body, restricted and narrowed the notion of the soul, since he reduced its content to thought alone, and assigned to its activity no other domain than the intellectual world of ideas.

The spiritualist philosophers who have succeeded Descartes have enlarged anew the somewhat narrow point of view occupied by the author of the *Discourse on Method*. They have restored to the soul the phenomena of sensibility, which Descartes was too much disposed to relegate to the lower regions of the organic life; consequently they speak again of the soul of animals, which, for Descartes, were no more than machines or automata.* Some of them have even gone so far as to attribute to the soul the phenomena of animal life and the physiological functions of the human body.[1]

27. The Soul and Psychological Facts. — These historical explanations were necessary in order to understand the direction of our studies and to define with exactness the domain of psychology.

It is not necessary at present to take sides for or against spiritualism. Our only concern is with facts immediately present to our consciousness.

The soul is not a fact of experience. It is a hidden

---

[1] This is the doctrine called *animism*, in opposition to vitalism, which admits a *vital principle* to explain the functions of life. It is now the general tendency to consider the organic functions as the result of purely material phenomena.

cause of which we know directly only the effects; an unknown substance of which we apprehend only the particular and successive modifications. But these effects, these modifications, to whatever principle we are hereafter to refer them, constitute a distinct and irreducible category of phenomena which ought to be the essential object of psychological research. The great number of contradictory conceptions of the soul, considered by some as the principle of thought alone, by others as a principle that feels, thinks, and wills, and by still others as the sole cause of life and thought, suffice to prove how very necessary it is to postpone, if not entirely to waive, the obscure and controverted question of the nature of the soul.

28. Consciousness the Limit of Psychology. — Psychological facts will therefore be defined as conscious facts, or at least as facts susceptible of becoming conscious. Consciousness is the natural limit of psychology. Whatever is known through consciousness — all the phenomena which succeed each other in our spiritual tribunal, instinctive or voluntary actions, sensations, or feelings, ideas or judgments, which sleep alone suspends or at least retards, and which, in order to be known, do not require the mediation of the senses, — all these are included within the domain of psychology; everything, on the contrary, which escapes consciousness, remains outside of psychology.

It is true that psychologists claim, and not without

reason, the study of certain unconscious phenomena, for example, those thousands of latent recollections which lie dormant in our mind, but which may be suddenly awakened by one circumstance or another; but these facts, actually unconscious, may from moment to moment reappear in the light of consciousness; they are, so to speak, only provisionally unconscious; while the phenomena of animal life, such as circulation, respiration, and digestion, are unconscious naturally and always; they would be unknown, they would remain buried in the mysterious night and the obscure depths of the organism, if the senses did not penetrate there to discover them.

29. Distinction between Psychological Facts and Physiological Facts. — The physical and the spiritual are so intimately united in human nature, they exercise such a profound influence upon one another, that the attempt has sometimes been made to absorb psychology, which studies the moral life of man, in physiology, which studies his physical life. Digestion, circulation, and respiration, it is said, are functions of the stomach, heart, and lungs, just as thought is the function of the brain. The two sciences, that which studies thought, and that which studies the brain, ought then to be fused into one; and psychology is nothing more than a chapter in physiology. Nothing of this kind can be done, for between psychological phenomena and physiological phenomena there is a radical opposition of a nature which makes all assimilation impossible.

In the first place, these two categories of phenomena
are not known in the same way. Retire into yourselves, and in your memory review all you have done
since you awoke. On the one hand, you have accomplished certain acts: you have made your morning
toilet; you have gone to school and then to your
classes ; you have opened your books ; you have heard
your teacher's lecture ; you have replied to his questions ; you have acquired new ideas by your senses or
by your reflection, or by the use of your memory you
have reviewed old ideas ; finally, you have experienced
from your studies emotions of pleasure or of pain, and
from your toil sensations of fatigue. Of all this you
have been immediately informed by your consciousness ; you have known what you thought, what you
felt, and what you willed to do. But, on the other
hand, while you were engaged in study you lived ;
your organic functions were accomplished ; your heart
beat, your blood circulated, and you knew nothing of
it ; your muscles contracted or relaxed, your nerves
vibrated, and you were not informed of it.

Consequently, how can you confound these two series
of phenomena, those which are immediately revealed to
you the moment they come into existence, and those of
which you are ignorant, although they are taking place
within you without interruption, —for example, the circulation of the blood, of which you would have had
absolutely no idea if you had lived before Harvey ? *

In the second place, physiological phenomena are all movements of matter, as the contraction of the muscles, the vibration of the nerves, etc. Psychological phenomena are perhaps the consequences of certain movements of cerebral matter; but in themselves they are anything but movements, and it is precisely for this reason that they escape all sense-perception.

"It were to little purpose," says a contemporary psychologist, "if, the brain having been indefinitely enlarged, we could there move about as in a mill; or, having become transparent like glass, our sight could traverse it from part to part. We would there see no more psychological phenomena than we see in a mill or in a sphere of crystal." [1]

Finally, and in the third place, psychological phenomena and physiological phenomena are in a sense independent of each other. Doubtless we do not find thought without life; we have never met with a thinking being who was not at the same time a living being. But, on the contrary, in sleep, for example, not to speak of madness, we observe that life is prolonged and the physiological phenomena maintained even when the psychological phenomena are almost totally interrupted.

We do not always dream, there is dreamless sleep; and in this case feeling, thought, will, — all for a time disappear; consciousness is extinct, while the physical functions pursue their course.

---

[1] See M. Rabier, *Leçons de Philosophie*, t. L p. 29. This is a remarkable and scholarly work, too scholarly, perhaps, for elementary study.

30. Relations between Psychology and Physiology. — However distinct the facts studied by physiology may be from those which are the objects of psychology, we are no longer living in a time when the relations between these two phenomena are called in question. To-day, who would think of repeating what Barthélemy Saint-Hilaire * wrote thirty years ago in his preface to the *Psychology* of Aristotle : * " I believe that physiology has no place in a treatise on psychology " ? No, psychological facts are connected with physical conditions; they depend, in part at least, on the organism. The philosopher who would forget this connection would be in great danger of forgetting what cerebral weariness might remind him of, in the very midst of his meditations, that the brain also plays a part in the labor of the intelligence. There is almost always an allowance to be made for physiological considerations in the analysis of the different operations revealed to us by consciousness.

31. Classification of Psychological Facts. — Although the facts of psychology have consciousness for their unique form, they differ greatly from one another, and the first care of the psychologist ought to be to classify them and to distribute them into categories according to their essential resemblances and differences.

32. The Faculties. — The classes of moral phenomena recognized by observation are designated as so many faculties. The faculties are to the soul what properties are to inanimate matter, or functions to organized bodies. They are the forces of the moral world.

No one would now think of doing what was formerly done, — take the faculties for independent and distinct entities,* for separate existences. The faculties are but general and abstract denominations, nominal labels, under which psychologists arrange for convenience of exposition the families of analogous facts which they have distinguished in the consciousness. It is to be clearly understood that every time we use the word *faculty* we shall comprehend under that term a collection of facts.

33. History of the Question. — Let us briefly recall the different schemes of classification which have been proposed for the moral faculties. Plato distinguished three parts in the soul: the intelligence or reason, the heart or courage, the source of noble or elevated passions, and desire or inferior sensibility. In the seventeenth century, with Descartes and his disciples, we see the faculties reduced to the understanding, or intelligence, and the will; sensibility is omitted. On the other hand, Bossuet * confounds the will and the understanding under the same class of intellectual operations, and establishes a class apart for the emotional activities.

It is in Germany, and in the last century among the psychologists of Wolf's * school, who really invented the word "psychology," up to that time unused, that there was established for the first time, with some degree of precision, the distinction, now classical and commonplace, of the three faculties, — the sensibility, the intelligence, and the will. Rejected by the sensualists who, like Condillac,* would see nothing in psychological phenomena but the transformations of a unique, primordial fact, which was sensation, the triple division of the moral faculties has been admitted by most other philosophers. Reid * and the Scotch school, it is true, returned to the Cartesian theory, and distinguished only the active faculties and the intellectual faculties. But more and more, and notwithstanding the isolated attempts of certain persons, who, like the phrenologists,* propose a classification much more complicated and much longer, the philoso-phers of the most diverse schools, the positivists* as well as the spiritualists, those who doubt the existence of the soul as well as those who believe in it the most firmly, are united in dividing mental science into three departments. Thus Alexander Bain,* one of the most celebrated representatives of contemporary English psychology, admits the three categories which he defines in these terms :

1. *Feeling*, which includes pleasures and pains. The words emotion, passion, and affection are synonyms of feeling.

2. *Volition*, or will.

3. *Thought*, intelligence, or knowledge. The sensa-

tions are arranged in part under feeling and in part
under thought.

**34. Facts Affective or Sensitive, Intellectual, or Voli-
tional.** — In order to comprehend the difference between
the three series of facts which are distinguished by
psychologists, the best way, perhaps, is to refer to the
personal experience of each one, and to go in quest of
examples.

The heat which the sun communicates, the perfume
which we inhale from flowers, the sweet taste of honey,
and, also, the emotion caused by the sight of a picture,
the sorrow felt on losing a friend, — these are sensations
and feelings. Notwithstanding the differences which
separate them, all these facts resemble one another in
that they are emotions, facts *affective* or *sensitive;*
they all have for a common characteristic that they
consist in loving or in hating, and consequently in
enjoying or in suffering.

On the other hand, the perception of the form or of
the color of an object, the recollection of a past event,
the image we retain of a monument or of a landscape,
the idea of a quality common to a great number of
persons, as wickedness or virtue, the demonstrations
of geometry, — these are *intellectual* facts, all of which
have this fundamental characteristic of being *representative*, of offering to the consciousness the representation either of an object or of some relation between
objects.

Finally, the acts which a man accomplishes when he speaks, when he sets himself to work, when he writes, when he changes his position, when he forms any resolution whatever, — these are facts, all of which have for their initial cause the *will*, or the power of self-determination to an action.

The first are connected with the sensibility, the second with the intelligence, and the last with the voluntary activity.

35. Table of the Faculties. — All the essential facts of the moral life are included within these three categories, *sensibility, intelligence, will.* These three attributes exhaust the definition of mind, which may be regarded as a force which feels, thinks, and wills; which is equivalent to saying that the human mind manifests itself successively through sensations or feelings, through thoughts, and through volitions.

However, in order to be rigorously complete, and by reason of the strict relations between body and mind, we must also include among psychological facts certain intermediate facts, mediating, so to speak, between mind and body, and placed on the confines of psychology and physiology, — these are the movements and the instincts, which may be connected with *physical activity.*

On the other hand, the phenomena of sensibility differ profoundly in their origin, in their objects, and in their order of evolution. The pleasures and the pains of the body, in a word, the sensations, are intimately connected with the physical organs ; while the joys and the sorrows of the heart and the mind are of a higher nature, are developed later, and presuppose, as antecedents, intellectual facts. The first constitute the *physical sensibility*, the other the *moral sensibility*, which should not be studied until after the intelligence, since it is in part derived from it.

In conclusion, the table of the psychological faculties may be divided as follows : —

1. PHYSICAL ACTIVITY.
2. PHYSICAL SENSIBILITY.
3. INTELLIGENCE.
4. MORAL SENSIBILITY.
5. VOLUNTARY ACTIVITY.

36. Relations of the Faculties to Each Other. — It is to be clearly understood, however, that in fact the different states of consciousness do not exist wholly isolated and are not absolutely independent of one another ; the faculties work together and aid one another ; the phenomena mingle and fuse together.

Thus the intelligence is associated with all psychological operations, since consciousness, which is the common characteristic of all these operations, is itself the chief of the intellectual functions. There is not a joy or a sorrow, an affection or an aversion, which is not conscious of itself, and which, in addition, does not implicate, in a greater or less degree, the idea of the object, agreeable or disagreeable, loved or hated, which provokes these emotions. And so there is no volition which does not presuppose the knowledge, vague or definite, of the act which we have resolved to accomplish, and the motives for which the resolution has been taken. It is rare that the mind exists in an exclusive state, but the classical division into three essential faculties still holds good, and the necessities of analysis require that psychology separate ideally and in theory what in reality is one.

The legitimacy of the distinction of the faculties, thus understood, can be doubted by no one; but we must be on our guard against attaching to this work of classification more importance than it deserves. A thing of greater interest to the psychologist is to describe and analyze facts for the sake of referring them, not only to the classes which comprise them, but to the laws which govern them.

SUMMARY.

1. **PSYCHOLOGY** is the study of the inner facts which constitute the moral life of man, as distinguished from his physical life.

2. **EMPIRICAL PSYCHOLOGY** is a science of facts. **RATIONAL PSYCHOLOGY** is a metaphysical science which attempts to connect these facts with some single principle, as the soul, according to the spiritualists.

3. The **SOUL** has been variously understood : as a principle of permanence and form in minerals ; as a principle of life in plants ; as a principle of sensibility and movement in animals ; and, finally, as a principle of thought in man.

The word "soul" has become more and more the synonym of the **SPIRITUAL PRINCIPLE** which feels, thinks, and wills.

4. The study of psychological facts is independent of the conclusions which philosophers reach concerning the existence and nature of the soul.

5. **PSYCHOLOGICAL FACTS** are distinguished from **PHYSIOLOGICAL FACTS** as follows : 1, They are immediately known through the consciousness ; 2, they are not, like physiological facts, simple movements of extended matter ; 3, they may not co-exist with physiological phenomena.

6. Psychological facts present resemblances and differences which allow us to classify them under a certain number of categories called the **FACULTIES OF THE SOUL.**

7. A faculty is nothing more than a complement of conscious states having the same nature.

8. We distinguish three series of psychological facts : 1, affective or sensitive facts ; 2, intellectual facts ; 3, volitional facts ; and consequently, three faculties : the **SENSIBILITY,** the **INTELLIGENCE,** and the **WILL.**

9. To these three essential faculties there must be added **PHYSICAL ACTIVITY.** As to the affective facts, they should be connected, some with physical sensibility, and others with moral sensibility.

CHAPTER II

PHYSICAL ACTIVITY: MOVEMENTS, INSTINCTS, HABITS

37. Evolution of the Faculties. — Man does not arrive at once at the full possession of his moral faculties. It is by slow degrees that he rises from animal life to human life. In the study of psychological phenomena, it is evidently best to follow this natural order of evolution. We shall therefore begin our inquiries, not with an analysis of the highest faculties, but with an examination of the humblest facts, those which are common to animals and men.

38. Activity in General. — Under this head it is physical activity which first presents itself to our observation. In a sense, it is true, every psychological operation is an act, a phenomenon of activity. To think, to feel, is also to act. Activity, under all its forms, may be defined as the development of a force which tends to a given end. But we give to the word "activity" a more restricted and definite signification when we regard it as the principle of actions which it manifests outside of itself, as when we employ the expression *physical activity* to designate the totality of influences or causes which determine the movements of the body.

Physical activity, at first blind, fatal, determined by obscure causes, by dull and almost unconscious instincts, passes thence under the domain of the sensibilities, that is, of the conscious emotions; and still later it comes under the empire of the will. But at all its stages and under all its forms, it may be defined as *the power of acting on the muscles and of producing corporeal movements.*

39. Movements in the Child. — The phenomena of movement are the first which manifest themselves in the child. Long before he thinks, he acts, he moves. As soon as he is born he becomes active and moves his lips for nourishment; he closes his eyelids to shield himself from the glare of too strong a light; he contracts the muscles of his chest and throat in order to cry or crow.

40. Are Movements Psychological Phenomena? — The movements of the body are above all physiological facts resulting from the play of nerve and muscle. But they are also, in part, psychological facts, — they will become so in proportion as they fall under the survey of consciousness. The child is not a simple machine, and his movements are not purely mechanical acts, the result of a material automatism.

41. Classification of Movements. — The ordinary movements of the child present themselves under many forms and participate more or less in the conscious life. Some of them are almost wholly unconscious.

We shall especially distinguish *spontaneous move-ments*, which proceed from nature itself, from an internal excitation, from *provoked movements*, which are determined by an exterior stimulus.

42. Spontaneous Movements. — In the adult, and in certain cases even in the child, the spontaneous movements have their cause in the will; they then depend upon the *volitional activity*, which we shall study farther on (Chapter XVI.). In this case, we produce a movement with the conception of cause fully before us, in order to accomplish a premeditated action or to attain a foreseen end. But before obeying our will, our nerves and muscles are obedient to blind necessity, to the unconscious tendencies of nature.

1. In a few cases, the movements of the child are caused by a habit already contracted in pre-natal life. Habit, that tyrant of life, already exercises its authority over the infant. The observers of infancy have proved, for example, that infants have a tendency to place their hands upon their face and eyes and to bend their limbs toward their body ; these are habitual movements.

2. Hereditary habits transmitted by parents may also determine special movements. Pérez observed a child of six days that lifted its hand mechanically to its face and succeeded in placing it on its head. The child's father recognized in this movement one of his own ordinary gestures.

3. But these are only exceptional cases and of but

little importance. A far greater number of move·
ments, in the child and even in the mature man, are
explained by the *spontaneous activity* of the *nerve centres*. There is in the child an energy of vital force, a
freshness and superabundance of overflowing vigor,
which manifests itself by disorderly gesticulation and
incessant mobility. The more powerful the vital functions, the more active the movements will be. At
every period of life the natural vigor of the organs and
the high health of the functions will be expressed by
movements of this class.

43. Provoked Movements — The movements of a
child and even of a man are not always the consequence of an interior and spontaneous excitation ; they
often proceed from an exterior cause. Such, for
example, are the brusque and sudden movements determined in us by the sight of a repulsive object, by a
startling noise, or by the sensation of tickling.

44. Reflex Actions. — The irreflective, involuntary
acts, provoked by an exterior agent, furnish us with a
perfect type of what the physiologists call a reflex
action, through analogy, doubtless, with the phenomena
of the reflection of light.

Reflex action is in some sort the response of the
living organism to the exterior excitation which solicits
it. The sensitive plant, when it folds its leaves at the
slightest touch, gives us the image of reflex action.
But reflex action really exists only in animals that have

a nervous system and a muscular system, the first susceptible of irritation and the second of contraction.
The two systems, the two tissues, are so connected
that the irritation of one involves the contraction of
the other, and so they determine a movement. The
excitation once communicated to the nerves propagates
itself along the nerve fibres and stops at a nerve centre,
whence it is transmitted to a muscle by means of
another nerve.

Of course, although the type of reflex action is a
provoked movement, spontaneous movements are also
reflex actions whenever they are unconscious and automatic. In this case the nervous excitation produces
itself by virtue of the native activity of the nerve centres. But reflex action is always and absolutely irreflective; consciousness is absent from it, and still more
the will. "Reflex actions," says Herbert Spencer, "are
but the aurora of the sensible life."

45. Instinctive Movements — We have just examined
different categories of movements, which have for antecedent or cause, either a habit, individual heredity, an
overflow of physical activity, or an exterior excitation.
But there is a whole series of spontaneous movements,
of much greater importance, that are to be explained
by instinct.

Instinctive movements are distinguished from other
spontaneous movements, by the fact that they are co-
ordinated, regular, and directed towards an end. But

they do not know this end, or they know it but faintly; they tend toward it almost blindly, and in this respect they are distinguished from voluntary movements.

Of this number are the movements which the infant accomplishes in order to take nourishment, to co-ordinate its eyes for seeing, and to give its limbs the locomotive rhythm.

46. Instinct in Man. — Certain philosophers assert that instinct is the prerogative of the animal. Capable of learning everything, man, it is said, begins by knowing nothing ; he does not have instinct, or has it only in a slight degree. In this respect human life, in which reflection plays a great part, is surely not to be compared with animal life, almost entirely enslaved to blind instinct. But in the early years of the child, at least, it is impossible not to recognize the fact that instinct is the source of a certain number of actions. Before man, who is expected to govern himself, is in full possession of his reason and his will, nature has placed him under the protection of certain dispositions which serve him as guides, which determine him to act, and to act in conformity with the essential needs of his existence.

47. Characteristics of Instinct. — Instinct may be defined as an innate tendency or impulse to act, which precedes all education, which supposes no previous reflection, but which nevertheless attains the end pursued with marvellous certainty.

Instinct is the part of man's nature which is the gift of heredity. Every individual owes his very existence and his ability to reproduce, in turn, the type of the species to which he belongs, to the fact that he is endowed with instincts.

The characteristics of instinct have often been described by philosophers, but in general they have been defined with an exactness too absolute.

Thus, it is affirmed that instinct is *unconscious*, and that it is characterized by an ignorance of the end which it pursues, and of the act which it accomplishes.

This is not true except with certain reservations. All instinct is not necessarily blind. We are not prepared, for example, to admit that in the child the instinct to take nourishment is absolutely deprived of consciousness. The intense delight so early manifested by the infant when it approaches its nurse's breast, is a proof that it is conscious, in some degree, from the first, of the satisfaction given to its need of nutrition.

And, again, it is said that instinct attains immediate and infallible perfection without study. More careful observation will prove, I think, that even bees and ants, in their marvellous constructions, do not entirely escape the need of feeling their way, but that even they are sometimes guilty of blunders.

It is truer to say that instinct is *special*, and that it applies itself to only one thing, to one determined end.

A bird does not construct every kind of nest, but a nest of a certain form.

48. How Far Instinct is Invariable. — Another characteristic of instinct, it is said, and the consequence of the preceding, is the absolute invariability or uniformity of the same actions, always identical throughout the centuries. The bees of Virgil and those of our day, we are told, construct their hives in the same manner. We do not deny that instinctive actions have a general resemblance ; but we believe they admit of a certain variability though it may be very limited.

Berthelot,* for example, relates that for a period of twenty-five years, he observed in the forest of Sèvres, a colony of ants, and that he there gathered undeniable facts which prove that animal societies are not absolutely immobile.

" I was able to observe," he says, "in my ant-hill, an emigration *en masse*. It was at the end of summer. The ant-hill, situated by a road frequented by pedestrians, had often been ravaged by their malevolent curiosity. Obliged again and again to reconstruct their dwelling-place, the ants finally became discouraged. One day, as I was passing over this road, I observed that it was traversed obliquely by a long column of ants. The next day, and the day following, the black column was in ceaseless march. Surprised at this perseverance, I followed the column. It moved toward the middle of the forest, not following any trail previously made by ants. It marched without division through dead leaves, weeds, and roots of trees, towards a spot evidently selected in advance. The march was three hundred metres in length. It ended amid trees at the foot of a shrub, on the top of a little sandy ridge of difficult approach and overlooking an old paved road. There a new ant-hill was in process of formation, partly below the surface, and in part above it. The emigration lasted the whole autumn. In the following spring the ancient village was deserted, but the new one was full of activity. But the new site had not been well chosen. If, by reason of its situation, it was out of the reach of pedestrians, it was, on the other hand, on the lower edge of a grassy slope over which water ran whenever it stormed. The ant-hill, flooded with water from time to time, never regained its early prosperity, but dwindled away, and after a few years completely disappeared, just as a city would have done that had often been ravaged by flood or pestilence."[1]

49. Conscious Movements. — If it is really true that there is some conscious, and hence psychological, element in instinctive acts ; if instinct supposes a certain degree of representation, however vague we may imagine it to be, of means to be employed, of an end to be reached ; it is true that instinctive movements involve consciousness only to slight degree. It is otherwise with certain movements that occur quite early in the child's life, and that are caused by his emotions ; as,

[1] Berthelot : *Science et Philosophie*, p. 176.

for example, when a child who is terrified starts suddenly backwards and conceals himself in the arms of
his nurse ; or when he experiences a feeling of pleasure
caused by seeing a luminous object, which his eye
follows as long as he can see it.

Here, doubtless, as in certain reflex actions, the
presence of an exterior object seems to be the cause of
a movement, while in reality it is only the occasion of
it.   In such cases there is not simply a transmission of
an external excitation which is communicated to nerves
and muscles ; but there is between the exterior agent
and the movement a conscious medium, fear, surprise,
some pleasure or pain ; so that in these cases the movement has for an antecedent, not merely a blind disposition, or a physical excitation, but a conscious operation,
a psychological fact.

50. The Beginning of Voluntary Activity. — The instinctive life in man is but an accident, a provisional
state, a regency, so to speak, which prepares for the
establishment of a permanent royalty, that of the
reflective will.   Through the mediation of instinct,
nature, as it were, holds the child by the hand till
the approaching moment when he can walk alone.
Thus, from the earliest period of life, the will tends
to disengage itself from instinct, and it is not long
before the first intentional movements begin to show
themselves.

The child early finds in his nascent desires the

starting-point of an activity wholly spontaneous, wholly conscious, which is a foreshadowing of the will.

Here is a child eight months old ; the moment his nurse takes him in her arms, in the morning, he at once pats her on the back to signify that he wishes to take a walk ; for before enjoying the pleasure of walking by himself, the child is very fond of walking as he is carried by others ; as his nurse approaches the door which he is to pass, he is in a flutter of excitement which is clearly significant. At the same age, the child is seen to move his head and his eyes in a given direction in order to find an object that he desires to see. If you conceal yourself near him he will readily bend, stoop, or turn, so as to find you. Consequently, at this age, the child has control of his little limbs and governs them ; he is their master. Not of them all, doubtless ; for all are not destined to become servants of the will. During our whole life, many acts which presuppose muscular movements, as respiration for example, will remain independent of our will. But, at least, the child has already acquired the possession of certain parts of the muscular system ; in his way he controls them as well as a grown man. And in maturity, as well as in infancy, desire, intention, and will, will continue to act upon the muscles and to produce regulated and concerted movements ; while consciousness never informs us how a given movement of the body follows the conscious intent.

51. How the Child Learns to Walk. — One of the great events in the life of a child is his first step. At the same time, it is one of the acts which best show that intermixture which characterizes human nature as distinguished from animal nature, — that perpetual intermingling of instinct with effort and of automatic and mechanical tendencies with conscious intent. Children spend much time in learning to walk. It has been observed that a child that is early in speaking is late in walking, and *vice versa*. This is probable, for nature hardly likes to make two efforts at once. What is certain is that locomotion is a real study for the child. The animal, on the contrary, often begins to frisk about at birth, and the bird flies almost the instant it comes from the egg. The child feels his way for a long time. At first he will raise himself on his mother's knees and will stiffen the muscles of his legs so as to keep upon his feet; then he will learn to make the alternate, the rhythmic movement which constitutes walking; and finally, he will dare to risk himself alone in space, and it is here that the intention manifests itself under the form of intense desire, of daring, and of the voluntary pursuit of an end. The child will make his first attempt by clinging to the hand or to the clothing of the one who leads him; he will try to balance himself upon his feet; finally, after some falls, he will advance all alone, fixing his eyes upon the person he wishes to reach, and consequently manifesting a voluntary effort. And the joy which beams in his eyes when he has thus conquered space is a clear proof of the intensity of his effort and of the feeling arising from the difficulty overcome.

52. Physical Habits. — It is not intentional effort alone, united with instinctive tendencies, that determines physical movements. Habit here plays a great part, and this from the earliest years of life. It is one of the essential laws of our nature that every act tends to reproduce itself for the sole reason that it has once been produced. We acquire a disposition to do over again what we have already done, and to do it the second time with greater facility and certainty. The intensity of the necessary effort decreases in proportion as the power of habit increases. In fact, habit has all the characteristics of instinct; but it is an acquired instinct, a second nature.

Walking, writing, musical execution, speech itself, all the movements which at first are based on instinct or on intentional effort, very soon become habitual acts to which we resign ourselves almost without thinking of them.

53. Physical Activity in the Mature Man. — It is particularly in the child that we have studied physical activity, because, in his case, it presents well-marked characteristics, because it is there more directly subject to organism and to instinct, and also because physical activity is nearly the whole of infant life. But during the whole period of life, physical activity remains one of the essential attributes of human nature. Only, with the progress of age, the part played by instinct diminishes, and physical actions depend more and more upon will and habit. We voluntarily place ourselves at our desk to write, but it is habit that guides our hand and places the letters upon the paper. We voluntarily decide to take a walk, but it is habit that guides our feet and determines the movements of our limbs.

But the physical activity of the man will in more than one case preserve the characteristics of the physical activity of the child. While we are engaged in the toil of thought, or in the reveries of the imagination, many gestures will escape us which will have no intentional cause, but which, like the mobility of the child, will be the result of the spontaneous excitation of the nerve centres.

SUMMARY.

10. **PHYSICAL ACTIVITY** is the power of acting upon the muscles and of producing bodily movements.

11. Before being voluntary and **CONSCIOUS**, physical activity is at first **FATAL** and **BLIND**; it is determined by obscure and unconscious causes, as the excitation of nerve centres, heredity, instinct, etc.

12. In the child the movements are either **SPONTANE-OUS** or **PROVOKED**. When they are unconscious they constitute what are called reflex actions.

13. REFLEX ACTIONS consist in a nervous excitation followed by a contraction of the muscles; the cause of the nervous excitation may be either an exterior impulse or a spontaneous impulse of the nerve centres.

14. The **INSTINCTS** are systems of reflex action; the movements which they determine are distinguished from other spontaneous movements in being prescribed, regulated, and directed toward an end; and they differ from spontaneous movements in being ignorant of the end toward which they tend.

15. However, **INSTINCTIVE MOVEMENTS** presuppose a certain representation of the means to be employed in order to reach a proposed end: they are neither as infallible nor as invariable as certain philosophers affirm.

16. CONSCIOUS MOVEMENTS, which arise from emotions of the sensibility, early manifest themselves in the child.

17. INTENTIONAL and **VOLUNTARY MOVEMENTS** are also displayed at an early period. The will plays a certain part, as, for example, in learning to walk.

18. Habit intervenes in physical activity, as in writing, in the execution of music, etc.

CHAPTER III

PHYSICAL SENSIBILITY: PLEASURE AND PAIN, SEN-SATIONS AND FEELINGS, WANTS AND APPETITES

54. Definition of Sensibility — With the sensibility, we actually enter the world of consciousness. There are, as we well know, unconscious movements; but an unconscious sensibility would be something incomprehensible, a pure contradiction in terms. A sensible being is necessarily conscious of what he feels. "I feel," is synonymous with "I am conscious of a sensation or of a feeling."

Common to animals and men in some of its manifestations, sensibility, under all its forms, may be defined as *the faculty of experiencing pleasure and pain, and, consequently, of loving and of hating.*

55. Different Meanings of the Word Sensibility. — Sensible or sensitive phenomena, in the precise language of psychology, are essentially agreeable or disagreeable phenomena which suppose, or, on the contrary, provoke, the existence of an inclination or of an aversion. They must not be confounded with the intellectual phenomena which generally accompany them, and which certain philosophers are wrong in connecting with the sensibility.

Thus the child opens his eyes to the light and sees the colors which charm his eyes and the appearance of which delights him. In this case, two very distinct phenomena are produced in him : the pleasure which the brilliant color procures for him, which is a fact of sensibility, and the perception, the knowledge of the color, which is a fact of intelligence. (See Chapter VI.)

56 Sensitive Facts and Intellectual Facts. — Sensitive facts and intellectual facts are thus distinguished from one another as follows : the first are purely *affective*, — they constitute an inner state of the soul, as pleasure or pain ; the second, on the contrary, are *representative*, — they teach us something about the nature of external objects.

Sensibility and intelligence are not merely *differences of nature*. Although they often co-exist, — the most of our pleasures and pains being accompanied by the representation of the object which causes them, — there are cases where the two faculties act separately and prove that they are independent of each other. Certain states of pain or indefinable discomfort affect our sensibility, and yet our intelligence may not know and not represent to itself the cause of them. The same thing is true of certain mysterious impressions of comfort and pleasure. On the other hand, the greater number of our intellectual representations appear to our consciousness without any intermixture of pleasure or pain. Whether it be the nature of the object, or the effect of the habit, we remain indifferent before the most of our thoughts. We study geometry without finding in it the pleasure which made Pascal * tremble in the presence of certain theorems.

57. Evolution of Sensibility. — Conscious in all its degrees, sensibility is nevertheless not always identical with itself. It extends from the humblest actions of animal life, from the phenomena of physical activity which we have already studied and with which it mingles pleasures and pains, up to the highest manifestations of the moral life which it saddens or embellishes with agreeable or painful emotions.

In the child, sensibility begins by associating itself with the functions of organic life. No doubt, the nursling, impelled by the need of nutrition, experiences an extreme pleasure in clinging to the breast of its mother. Later on, sensibility connects itself with the representations of the exterior world of which the five senses are the source ; there are pleasures of seeing, hearing, etc. Later still, sensibility, emerging from ourselves and reaching beyond selfishness, attaches us to animals or to our fellows. A child smiles upon its mother, and its smile is the expression of its affection. Finally, when the intelligence is ripe for abstract ideas, the sensibility allows itself to be moved by these ideas. A train of sweet or painful emotions accompanies the most elevated thoughts ; our heart beats for justice, for truth, for native land.

58. Physical Sensibility and Moral Sensibility. — Sensibility will therefore vary according to the nature of the causes which excite it, or the objects which provoke it.

At one time, the sensitive phenomenon has for immediate antecedent or cause an organic need, as the need of eating, — a physical impression, the contact of a soft body ; and in this case it is called a *sensation*, and we connect it with *physical sensibility.*

At another time, on the contrary, pleasures and pains will have for their object, and consequently for their antecedent or cause, an idea or conception of the mind, a moral phenomenon ; for example, the idea of a fault which causes the pain of remorse, or the idea of a beautiful act which engenders the pleasure of admiration ; and then they are called feelings, and are to be connected with the *moral sensibility.*

59. Sensations and Feelings. — Sensations, consequently, may be defined as pleasures or pains which immediately follow a material phenomenon : for example, a burn, some lesion of the organs, the pleasure of walking, the satisfaction of the needs of nutrition, etc.

The feelings, on the contrary, are the pleasures and the pains which have for immediate antecedent a psychological phenomenon or intellectual representation : as the idea of our virtues or of our faults, giving rise to the pleasures and the pains of self-love ; or the idea of our parents or of our friends, giving rise to family

affection, the joys of friendship, etc. "The sensations," says Sully,* "proceed from nervous excitation;
the feelings, on the contrary, depend on one of the
forms of mental activity."[1]

It results from this difference of origin that the sensations may always be localized in a part of the body,
or in the organ where the need is manifested or the impression is produced: for example, I have the headache
or a pain in the stomach; I have burned my arm, or my
hand is agreeably affected by warmth or by cold. The
feelings, on the contrary, are not localized in the body.
It is by a simple figure of speech that common language
asserts that the heart is the seat of the feelings, by
reason, doubtless, of the brisker movement which the
emotions of the sensibility impress on the movement of
the blood and the beating of the heart.

We now understand why the study of physical
sensibility may and should precede the study of the
intelligence; while the study of moral sensibility, of
which we shall not speak till later (see chapters XIV.
and XV.), supposes a previous knowledge of intellectual
phenomena.

60. Different Designations of Sensitive Phenomena. —
The phenomena of sensibility play so large a part in
human life, and present so many complications and
delicate shades, that common language has multiplied
expressions and words, that are almost synonymous, to

[1] Teacher's Handbook of Psychology, New York, 1886.

designate their various forms. Before going farther, let us put a little order into this usual vocabulary of the sensibility.

Pleasures and joys are properly distinguished as follows : the first are physical pleasures ; the latter, pleasures of the soul : — the pleasures of taste and smell; family joys, and the joys of friendship.

The term emotions, brought into use by the English psychologists, may be applied to all the phenomena of the sensibility, physical and moral ; it is synonymous with sensitive facts.

Passions express a violent pursuit of pleasure, — dominant and exclusive inclinations.

Finally, appetites and propensities, inclinations and affections, are different words that designate the tendencies of the sensibility ; the first toward material good ; the last toward moral good : — the first toward selfish satisfaction ; the last toward disinterested satisfaction.

61. The Essential Elements of Every Sensitive Phenomenon. — Whatever may be their difference in origin and nature, the sensations and the feelings present to us the same essential phenomena : —

    1. INCLINATIONS OR AVERSIONS.
    2. PLEASURES AND PAINS.

Every sensation, every feeling, is at once an inclination or an aversion for a given object, and an impression of pleasure or of pain; so that the general theory of sensibility is the same for sensations and for feelings.

62. Pleasure and Pain. — It is not proposed to define pleasure and pain; they are simple elementary phenomena irreducible to any other, which every one knows sufficiently through his own experience.

But if it is impossible and useless to define these states of consciousness, it is necessary to explain them, that is, to make known their causes.

63. Pleasure and Inclination. — The cause of pleasure is nothing but the inclination or tendency to act in one way or in another. On the contrary, it is sometimes said that inclination is the effect of the pleasure felt; and it is very certain that a consequence of the pleasure is to heighten the inclination and to give it full consciousness of itself. We have no decided inclination for hunting until after having tasted the pleasures of hunting, for play until after having played, nor for tobacco until after having smoked. But it is none the less true that every pleasure supposes a previous inclination, a natural tendency, conscious or unconscious; conscious when the need or the desire precedes the action; but often unconscious, though not less real, when it reveals itself only through the very pleasure which is experienced in satisfying it. In the child still inexperienced, pleasure often precedes inclination, and a skilful teacher may thus inspire him with tastes which he never suspected.

Pleasure is then an inclination that is satisfied; and pain, an inclination that is opposed.

64. The Laws of Pleasure and Pain. — Let us take examples to illustrate the relations of inclination with pleasure and pain.

We have a tendency or inclination to walk; and if we walk moderately, without going beyond our strength, we experience pleasure; but if the walk is prolonged, if it is a forced march, we have a sense of fatigue and of discomfort. We naturally love light and colors; and a mild light and vivid colors impress us agreeably; but a dazzling light or a loud color offends us and makes us suffer.

We have a natural taste for reading and study; but just as reading and study refresh and delight us when we apply ourselves to them in moderation; so we experience pain if we impose them forcibly, or for too long a time, upon our jaded mind.

It follows from these examples, selected out of thousands, that pleasure is the natural consequence of the moderate and appropriate exercise of each of the organs of our body, or of each of our spiritual faculties. A moderate action of the senses, of the muscular energies, or of the mental faculties, is accompanied with pleasure.

If, on the contrary, the action goes beyond certain limits, the pleasure insensibly diminishes and is soon changed into discomfort and then into pain.

Aristotle had already observed this : —

"It is in action," he said, "that comfort and happiness consist. Pleasure is not the act itself, nor an intrinsic quality of the act; but it is an adjunct which never fails it, it is a final perfection added to it, as bloom to youth. Each action has its own pleasure."

"Pleasure," says Hamilton,* "is the reflex of the spontaneous and unimpeded exertion of a power, of whose energy we are conscious. Pain, a reflex of the over-strained or repressed exertion of such a power." [1]

65. Consequences of these Laws. — In the light of these explanations, almost all the so-called caprices of the sensibility become simple and clear; all its mysteries vanish.

Why, for example, does novelty always please us, while uniformity irritates and wearies us? Because new things excite and call into play our surplus energies, accumulated during inaction; while these same energies are used up by exercises too prolonged or too frequently repeated.

Why were we charmed yesterday by what displeases us to-day? Because, the object remaining the same, our personal dispositions have changed. Yesterday we were ready for action, for brain work, for walking; while to-day we are no longer ready for them.

Why has idleness so much attraction for some, while others find happiness only in action? It is because all minds have not the same surplus of energy; it is

1 Sir William Hamilton: *Lectures on Metaphysics*, p. 575.

because intellectual activity, which for some is the natural and easy display of the exuberant powers of the intelligence, is for others but constrained labor out of proportion to their resources. Moreover, the idle are afflicted with *ennui* when they cannot apply themselves to some favorite occupation.

Why, again, are some objects always disagreeable, as black to the eyes and rhubarb to the taste? Because the sensations which result from them have a tendency to oppose or to suppress the normal activity or natural exercise of our faculties; for example, black gives to the organ of vision a sort of immobility or inactivity.

But we are not to forget that pain does not result alone from excessive action; it is also the consequence of forced inaction. There are negative pains, as privation of light, or prolonged solitude, or immobility.

There are positive pains, as excessive heat or violent effort. Between these two extremes, at an equal distance from inaction and an excess of activity, appears pleasure, the consequence of a medium activity, or, rather, of an activity directed in accordance with nature, conforming to our natural aims, and, at the same time, adjusted to the strength at the disposal of the individual.

66. Correlation of Pleasure and Pain. — The correlation of pleasure and pain is also a consequence of the laws which we have just stated. Socrates * related that pleasure and pain were at first irreconcilable enemies, but that Jupiter, in order to re-establish peace, had united them by bands of gold, so that, like two companions in chains, they follow one another. And, in fact, the discomfort of hunger or thirst is followed by the pleasure of eating and drinking; and every privation, which is a suffering, is followed, the moment it ceases, by pleasure and enjoyment. Likewise, excessive pleasure engenders satiety, which is accompanied by discomfort. However, we do not believe, with certain psychologists, that the conscious life is an uninterrupted series of pleasures and pains. Whatever may be said to the contrary, there are neutral or indifferent states.[1]

67. What Lies at the Basis of Inclination. — We explain pleasure by saying that it is the satisfaction of an inclination; but the inclination itself, how are we to explain it?

Inclination is the natural tendency to act in one direction or in another, and consequently to seek and to love whatever is in accordance with our activity, whatever is good; and to shun and detest whatever is contrary to it, whatever is evil.

Inclination is activity *canalized*, so to speak, by nature in different directions.

In a sense we must say that the basis of inclination is love, the love of whatever promotes the conservation and development of our being.

---

[1] To prove that man is never "in a neutral state without joy or sorrow," F. Marion is obliged to admit "unconscious joys and sorrows," which is a pure contradiction. *Leçons de Psychologie*, p. 219.

At first unconscious, love instinctively seeks whatever is agreeable to it. When it once possesses this
it experiences pleasure ; and this pleasure, once felt,
leaves in the consciousness the desire to find the
agreeable object again.

Desire is the conscious inclination which knows
what it loves ; it is the recollection of a past pleasure
and the aspiration for a new pleasure of the same
kind.

68. Classification of the Emotions. — Inclination and
pleasure form a whole, an aggregate which by a single
word we may call emotion. We have already seen that
the emotions are to be classed under two great categories, the *sensations* and the *feelings*.

The sensations or emotions of physical sensibility are
themselves subdivided into two classes : 1, the emotions which are connected with the organs of material
life, and which depend upon the accomplishment of
their functions: these are called *wants, or appetites ;*
2, the emotions which result from the exercise of the
five senses, taste, smell, hearing, sight, and touch :
these are the *pleasures of sense.*

69. The Appetites. — The wants or appetites are the
inclinations of the organic life. There are as many
wants or appetites as there are distinct functions in the
organism.

The characteristics of the appetites are those of all
the sensations. Appetite is always preceded by a

physiological phenomenon, by an organic modification; hunger and thirst correspond to a particular state of the digestive tracts; consequently appetite is localized in a part of the body.

Certain appetites are distinguished from other sensations by their *periodicity*. Satisfied for a time, and appeased by satiety, they reappear at definite intervals, when, on the demand of the functions for renewed activity, the want reappears: for example, the want of nourishment, the want of sleep.

70. Classification of the Appetites. — The list of appetites is as long as the list of organic functions.

The *functions* of *nutrition* (digestion, respiration, circulation, etc.) give rise to the appetite of hunger and thirst, which procure for us very keen enjoyment, and also the disagreeable sensations of nausea, of loathing, and of inanition. From the same source arise the need of warmth and the need of breathing; but this last want is so permanent and so regularly satisfied by nature that we do not feel the pleasure resulting from it; but, on the contrary, we experience discomfort and distress when this need is opposed, as in suffocation.

To the functions of relation correspond the need of movement and a correlative need of repose and sleep.

71. The Pleasures of the Senses. — The exercise of the five senses gives rise to appropriate pleasures of a higher order than the preceding. These pleasures, though rightly credited to the physical sensibility, are susceptible of modification under the action of the intelligence. The pleasures of sight become one of the essential sources of the æsthetic emotions, which we gain through the beautiful as realized in painting; and the pleasures of hearing are associated with the feelings awakened by music.

The pleasures of the five senses are, moreover, distinguished from the pleasures of the organic life, in being, so to speak, disinterested; they do not result from the necessary satisfaction of a need essential to existence; they mediate between the material necessities of the animal life and the noble and elevated contemplations of the intellectual life.

72. Intrinsic Characteristics of the Pleasures. — Each pleasure and each pain is a special phenomenon, *sui generis*, irreducible to any other. The pain caused by a burn does not resemble the pain caused by a headache; nor the pleasure excited by beautiful colors, the pleasure given by the audition of agreeable sounds. There are then as many species of pleasures and pains as there are of inclinations.

However, psychologists have attempted to distinguish the pleasures into several classes, according as they are *transient* or *durable*, *noble* or *low*.

This last distinction is the only one that deserves to be retained. Indeed, the emotions differ from each other according to the end toward which they tend. Distinct in their origin, they are also distinct in their aim. We could not place in the same rank in the moral hierarchy, the pleasures which tend merely to the conservation of material well-being, and those which, proceeding from the moral sensibility, tend to the development of our intellectual faculties.

73. Physical Sensibility in the Animal, in the Child, and in the Man. — Physical sensibility is common to animals and men. All living flesh is penetrated with sensibility; every organ is the seat of a need or tendency; every physical function is the source of enjoyment or of suffering.

But the intellectual faculties, more developed in man, impress on his physical sensibility particular characteristics; memory and reflection render human emotions more durable and more intense.

As between the child and the man, physical sensibility also presents notable differences. It is more acute in the child, first, because it is developed almost alone, and because neither moral sensibility nor intellectual reflection as yet intervenes to curb its vigor. The child is wholly absorbed in his physical joys and griefs. He throws into his laughter and into his tears an accent which attests the intensity of his emotions. Later, his preoccupations, the effort of his thought and will, will modify the impressions of the senses; the mature man will enjoy less and suffer less in his appetites and in his senses. Probably nothing equals the intense joy of the first step or the first look. This difference is due also to the influence of habit. New and fresh, the emotions of the child are necessarily stronger ; in the mature man they tend to grow dull.

SUMMARY.

19. The **SENSIBILITY** is the faculty of experiencing pleasure or pain, and consequently of loving or hating.

20. **SENSITIVE FACTS** are distinguished from intellectual facts in being **AFFECTIVE; INTELLECTUAL FACTS** are **REPRESENTATIVE**.

21. Sensitive facts have for antecedent, either a physiological fact or a psychological fact ; in the first case they are called **SENSATIONS**, and in the second, **FEELINGS**. The sensations constitute the physical sensibility; the feelings the moral sensibility.

22. **MORAL SENSIBILITY**, which presupposes the intelligence, ought not to be studied until after the intelligence.

23. The **SENSATIONS** are localized in an organ or in the part of the body where there is produced the physiological fact which precedes them.

24. In sensation, as in feeling, we discover the constituent elements of sensibility : 1, pleasure and pain ; 2, inclination.

25. **PLEASURE** always supposes a previous inclination, either conscious or unconscious.

26. **PLEASURE** is a **SATISFIED INCLINATICN; PAIN**, a **THWARTED INCLINATION**.

27. Pleasure results from a medium activity, in conformity with nature and adjusted to the powers at the disposal of the individual. Pain results either from forced inaction or from excessive action.

28. At bottom, **INCLINATION** is nothing but the love of the good, — the pursuit of individual conservation and development.

29. The **SENSATIONS**, or emotions of the physical sensibility, are divided into two categories: 1, the appetites; 2, the pleasures of the five senses.

30. The **APPETITES** correspond to the different functions of the organic life.

31. **THE PLEASURES OF THE SENSES** are intermediate between the physical sensibility and the moral sensibility.

CHAPTER IV

THE INTELLIGENCE IN GENERAL. DIVISION OF INTELLECTUAL FACTS

74. Definition of the Intelligence. -- The intelligence is the complement of facts by means of which we represent to ourselves either an object, or the relation between two or more objects. Considered as the principle of all these facts, it may be defined as the *faculty of thinking*. In fact, to think is the same thing as to know and to comprehend. To know is to represent to one's self a given object ; to comprehend is to grasp the relation between one object and another.

Etymologically, the intelligence (from the Latin verb *intelligo*) signifies exclusively the faculty of comprehending. But it is more exact to assign to it also the simple facts of knowledge. The sense-knowledge of exterior things, as the perception of a color or of a sound, although derived from the senses, is yet at the same time an intellectual fact.

75. The Relation of the Intelligence to the Other Faculties. — We cannot be too thoroughly convinced of the truth that psychological phenomena, whatever their diversity, are ever tending to mingle and combine.

Psychological analysis alone distinguishes and separates them, just as chemical analysis separates a compound body into its simple elements.

In the living reality of the consciousness there is not a single fact of the sensibility which is not accompanied by an intellectual fact ; there is at least the conscious-ness of pleasure or of pain, or the knowledge of the object which provokes the inclination or the aversion. And so the will always supposes an intellectual fact ; to will is to determine ourselves towards an action which we know ; it is to tend toward an end which we represent to ourselves.

Let us note that the intelligence alone, as distin-guished from the other faculties, is capable of independ-ent development, — it need not involve any sensitive or volitional fact in its activity. Doubtless the thinker is absolutely independent neither of the sensibility nor of the will. In his meditations, Descartes was very often sustained in his thoughts by the pleasure he found in them, and especially by his will, which imposed on him a law to pursue his course of reasoning. Usu-ally, thinking does not proceed without a secret enjoy-ment of spirit, nor without an intense attention ; but attention is the will directing the intelligence. In cer-tain cases, however, we judge and reason without add-ing any emotion to our judgments and reasonings, without having need of effort and will in order to pur-sue our thoughts. The geometrician who pursues the demonstrations of his theorems is but pure thought, he acts only intellectually.

76. The Understanding. — The word *intelligence* is now sanctioned by usage to designate all the facts which have the common characteristic of being thoughts. The word "understanding," formerly much employed, is adapted to designate only the highest acts of the intelligence, those which do not require the co-operation of the five senses.

The physicist who observes the qualities of bodies is engaged in the work of intelligence; but he is employing his understanding when he reasons in order to establish physical laws, or to explain the phenomena of nature. The geometrician who is incessantly reasoning is making constant use of his understanding.

The ancient philosophers sharply distinguished sense-operations, as sense-perception, memory, and imagination, from intellectual operations, such as generalization, judgment, and reasoning; and only the latter were referred to the understanding. It seems more just to include under one category all the facts of thought, whatever may be their source, — whether they are derived from sense-perception, or from a subsequent travail and proper elaboration of the mind.

77. Evolution of the Intelligence. — The intelligence manifests itself in the child from the day when he knows his mother, or when he distinguishes the objects which his senses present to him. But enveloped at first in the impressions of sense, the intelligence is developed little by little ; or, rather, facts of another order succeed the first perceptions of the senses. Preserved by the memory, the particular representations which are gradually accumulated in the mind give rise to comparisons from which are insensibly disengaged abstract or general ideas, which no longer represent particular objects, but their relations.

In other terms, the intelligence, which is at first but the mirror of things, gradually acquires its proper vitality.

It reacts on the elements of knowledge which are furnished it by sense-perception and by consciousness ; takes possession of them, modifies them, transforms them, rises to the highest conceptions ; and by reasoning gives extension to the primitive knowledge.

In a word, the mechanism of the intelligence supposes both data or original matter, and an action exercised by the intelligence itself in order to make use of these elementary data and to transform this original matter.

78. The Innate in the Intelligence. — The intelligence is not merely a vase which is gradually filled with the knowledge which the senses and the consciousness are daily pouring into it ; but it is a self-existing force which has its own tendencies, instincts, and its inflexible laws.

Not only does each intelligence derive from heredity

and its own nature greater or less vivacity, power, and aptness better to comprehend a given order of truths; but every intelligence, from the simple fact of being an intelligence, carries with it, from the first, principles which direct all its operations.

These principles constitute what is called the *reason*, that is, all that is innate in intelligence, as distinguished from *experience*, that is, from all that is acquired.

79. The Elements of the Intelligence : Idea and Judgment. — However diverse the forms of the intelligence, we find the same elements in all its manifestations. The elementary intellectual fact is the representation, or, in other terms, the idea : either a sensible and particular idea, as a man, a tree ; or an abstract and general idea, as humanity, vegetables, etc.

But ideas simply by themselves do not constitute the life of the spirit, the activity of the intelligence. The intelligence truly acts only when it associates ideas, that is, when it judges, when it affirms ; and, in fact, it is always judging. Judgment is the fundamental act of the intelligence ; it is to thought what respiration is to the body.

If there were but isolated ideas succeeding each other in the mind without some bond to associate them, the mind would be like a dictionary of words containing a list of all the substantives and adjectives in the language. In order that these words may have a value, they must be joined one to another, they must be united by the verb *to be*. So likewise, in order that the intelligence may act, ideas must be united one with another in order to form judgments which language translates into propositions or sentences.

80. Judgment the Essential Act of the Intelligence. — Let us take the different intellectual facts one by one, and we shall discover that they all consist in judging.

External perception, even under its most elementary form, is the affirmation at least of the existence of the object perceived. I affirm or I judge that this color exists or that I hear this sound. In a higher degree, external perception is the affirmation of the relation which I detect between two sensible ideas : this table is square, this flower is red.

The consciousness or inner perception is but the series of judgments which we form on the facts that take place within us. *I feel a pain*, is equivalent to this judgment : *I affirm that I feel a pain.* To have the consciousness of psychological phenomena is nothing else than to affirm their existence.

Memory is also a collection of judgments : I judge that I once saw such a person, or that two days ago I took such a walk.

Imagination itself terminates in judgments, and the ideas which it suggests to us have no significance unless they are united one to another. The landscape which I imagine is green ; the shade contributes to its freshness.

The reason has often been defined as the faculty of ideas and first truths. Now truth is but a judgment, a judgment in conformity with reality.

Abstraction and generalization are in a sense but the sources of abstract and general ideas; but these ideas never present themselves separately save in dictionaries; in the mind they are always combined with each other or with particular ideas in order to form judgments. "The Frenchman" (general idea) "is malicious" (another general idea). "I love" (particular idea) "humanity" (general idea). Finally, reasoning is nothing but a succession of judgments connected in such a way that the mind on comparing them derives from them a new judgment.

81. Division of Intellectual Facts. — Nothing is more varied than intellectual facts; hence, nothing is more complicated than their division and classification.

This diversity in intellectual facts occurs in various ways: first, by reason of the nature of the objects which the intelligence represents to itself (the material qualities of external objects, or the phenomena of spirit); next, according as the intelligence acquires its knowledge for the first time (perception), or has only to preserve it (memory); then, according as the intelligence derives its ideas from itself (reason), or receives them from experience (sense and consciousness); and lastly, according as the intelligence is simply the mirror in which objects are reflected, or as it becomes the active agent which elaborates the materials furnished by the primary faculties (abstraction, generalization, reasoning).

82. General Scheme of the Intellectual Functions. — In view of the different considerations which we have just indicated we offer the following classification of the facts and functions of the intelligence : —

1. *Functions of Acquisition,* also called the faculties of intuition, of immediate perception, or of experience : namely, the *senses* and the *consciousness.* The senses are as the windows of the house inhabited by the intelligence ; consciousness is the light which illumines the interior of the dwelling.

2. *The Functions of Conservation.* — These preserve or hold the knowledge furnished by the senses and by consciousness, or the knowledge which results from the subsequent functions of the intelligence. They are the *memory* and the *representative imagination.*

3. *The Functions of Elaboration and of Combination.* — These appropriate the materials or data of the consciousness and the senses, compare them, associate them by an effort of reflection, and by means of this elaboration succeed in constituting the intelligence. They are the *creative imagination, abstraction, generalization, and reasoning.*

The *reason* has not been mentioned in this scheme, because, in truth, it is not a particular function of the intelligence ; it is the intelligence itself in its native

constitution and innate laws. The reason dominates
all the intellectual operations ; it is the reason which
directs them and makes them possible.

83. Analysis of a Page of Descartes. — A very useful
exercise for leading us to recognize the different intellectual functions consists in analyzing some author's
train of thoughts.

Let us take, for example, a page of Descartes : —

" In my younger days I had studied logic as a branch of
philosophy, and geometrical analysis and algebra as branches
of mathematics, three arts, at least, which it would seem
could contribute something to my purpose " (*memory : Descartes recollects what he studied while young*).   " But on examining them " (*attention, analysis*), " I came to the conclusion
that as to logic, its syllogisms and the most of its other directions serve to explain to another the things which he already
knows rather than to teach him what is new " (*judgment :
Descartes asserts that logic is not useful for the discovery of
truth*).   " And though it contains many very true and excellent precepts, there are nevertheless so many others scattered among them that are either mischievous or superflu-
ous " (*abstract and general ideas*), " that it is almost as difficult
to separate them as to extract a Diana or a Minerva from a
block of marble which has not been touched by the chisel "
(*imagination : Descartes represents to himself the work of the
sculptor fashioning a statue*).   " Then, — as to the analysis of
the ancients and the algebra of the moderns, besides the fact
that they are applicable only to very abstract matters, the
first is always so restricted to the consideration of diagrams

that it cannot exercise the understanding without greatly
wearying the imagination. And in algebra we are so tied
down to certain rules that we have made of it a confused
and obscure art which embarrasses the mind, rather than a
science which cultivates it. This is what caused me to
think that I must look for another method, which, compris-
ing the advantages of these three, might be exempt from all
their defects " (*deductive reasoning: Descartes' syllogism might
be formulated as follows: — Major premise: the human mind
needs a method; Minor premise: logic, geometry, and algebra are insufficient methods; Conclusion: we must therefore
seek for a new method*). "And as the multiplicity of laws
often furnishes excuses for crime, so that the state is best
governed when it has a very few laws which are strictly
observed; so in place of the great number of precepts of
which logic is composed I think I would be satisfied with the
four following" (*inductive reasoning by analogy: Descartes
having observed what takes place in governments where
affairs are much better regulated where the laws are few,
concludes that it is also wise to reduce the laws of logic to a
small number*).

Save examples of sense-perception, which naturally
occur but very seldom in the abstract meditations of a
philosopher, the page which we have just analyzed
presents to us almost all the varieties of intellectual
labor.

If we wish really to enter into ourselves and to take
account of the operations which succeed one another

in our consciousness during a quarter of an hour of reflection, we will find with the same facility, in the fabric of our thoughts, the different threads which compose it ; some of which are borrowed from outward perception, some from the memory, some from the imagination, and some from the purely intellectual operations of abstraction and generalization.

84. Conditions of the Development of the Intelligence. — First of all, the intelligence presupposes material or data ; it will be rich in proportion as the senses have been well employed, as they have gathered up from our environment an abundance of notions or ideas, and as the living consciousness has revealed to us a copious supply of inward impressions. Guiding principles are also necessary to the intelligence ; and they are assured to man by his very nature, by his native constitution, and by his prerogative of reason. But in order to guarantee the development of the intelligence, certain other conditions are required which are not always realized.

85. Physiological Conditions : the Brain and Thought. — General physical health is of importance in the development of thought ; sound thought is generally connected with a sound body. Relations still more intimate exist between the intelligence and the brain. The brain is evidently the organ of thought, just as the eye is the organ of vision. We would not say that the brain is the principle of the intelligence ; but in the actual state of human nature it is the indispensable instrument of the intelligence. The loss of certain parts of the brain is followed by the disappearance of certain intellectual functions : just as the lack of certain keys of a piano prevents the musician from producing certain notes.

The progressive development of the intelligence, from infancy to maturity, corresponds exactly with the development of the brain.

"The brain," says an English psychologist, "like all other parts of the organism, *grows* in bulk or size, and *develops* or manifests certain changes in its formation or structure. The two processes, growth and development, do not progress with the same degree of rapidity. The size nearly attains its maximum about the end of the seventh year, whereas the degree of structural development reached at this time is not much above that of the embryonic condition." [1]

86. Psychological Conditions : Attention. — But if the development of the intelligence has its physical conditions, it depends also, and perhaps in a still higher degree, on psychological conditions ; and the chief of these is attention.

The attention was not given a place in the scheme of intellectual functions, because it is really not one of the particular faculties of the intelligence ; but it is the condition of the development of them all. To instinct-

[1] Sully : *Outlines of Psychology*, London, 1884, p. 54.

ive thought, which of itself will not proceed very far, there succeeds, by virtue of the attention, reflective thought. The lowest intellectual functions, external perception, for example, attain their full power only through the attention ; observing and listening are something more than seeing and hearing. As to the higher operations of the mind, they would hardly be possible without attention. Doubtless, when the process of reasoning has once been started, it may perhaps continue without effort, conducted by the simple impetus of thought ; but at least at the beginning of our meditations, we have need of attention in order to escape the yoke of sense-impressions and the fancies of the imagination, and to direct our thought towards the object of our researches.

SUMMARY.

32. The **INTELLIGENCE**, that is, the aggregate of intellectual facts, may be defined, the **FACULTY** of **THINKING**, that is, of knowing and comprehending, of knowing things and comprehending truths.

33. The intelligence accompanies all the operations of the sensibility, since all these operations are at least conscious of themselves. It is the principle or basis of will, since the will presupposes the knowledge of what is willed.

34. In its turn, the intelligence is supported by the pleasure which accompanies the act of thought, and by the will,

which is the basis of attention. However, there are intellectual facts absolutely independent of the sensibility and the will.

35. Intelligence is a word more comprehensive than **UNDERSTANDING**, which designates only intellectual operations, as **ABSTRACTION** and **REASONING**. It comprehends the operations of sense, as **PERCEPTION, MEMORY**, and **IMAGINATION**, as well as the intellectual operations.

36. Intelligençe has for a starting-point **SENSE-PER-CEPTION** and **CONSCIOUSNESS**, in a word, **EXPERIENCE**. With these materials, and by a subsequent effort, it forms **ABSTRACT IDEAS** and **GENERAL IDEAS**; it gives extension to its primitive knowledge through the process of **REASONING**, and is aided in all its operations by the **REASON**.

37. In all intellectual facts we discover the same elements, namely, **IDEAS**, that is, the representations of things. These ideas themselves are always associated one with another by an act of affirmation which constitutes the **JUDGMENT**.

38. All the intellectual functions terminate in judgments.

39. Intellectual facts are distributed under three great categories : —

(1) **FACTS OF ACQUISITION**, outward perception of the senses, inward perception of the consciousness.

(2) **FACTS OF CONSERVATION**, memory and representative imagination.

(3) **FACTS OF COMBINATION AND ELABORATION**, the creative imagination, abstraction, generalization, and reasoning.

40. The **REASON** is not a special intellectual function; it is the intelligence itself in its native constitution and its innate principles.

41. The intelligence, while borrowing its data from experience, and its laws from reason, still has need for its own development of certain conditions, some physical and physiological, as the **BRAIN**; the others, psychological, the principal of which is **ATTENTION**.

CHAPTER V

CONSCIOUSNESS AND ATTENTION

87. Consciousness and Attention. — Consciousness being the general form of all the intellectual facts, it must necessarily be studied first.

The same thing is true of attention, which in reality is but reflective consciousness, and of which we have already remarked that it constitutes the most important condition of intellectual development.

Every psychological fact is conscious, that is to say, it knows itself the very moment when it is produced. On the other hand, every intellectual function, after having been accomplished at first spontaneously, may be reproduced with reflection, that is to say, under the power of the attention.

It is therefore necessary, before examining the particular operations of the mind, to consider their common character and also their reflective mode, namely, consciousness and attention.

88. Conscience and Consciousness. — The word *conscience* has a moral signification. A good conscience is the moral state of an honest soul ; and a bad conscience, of a dishonorable soul. Philosophy also employs the word in the same sense. Conscience, for the moralist, is the aggregate of feelings and judgments which are connected with morals; it is the idea of the good and of duty ; it is repentance and remorse.

On the other hand, *consciousness* may be defined as the *knowledge which we have of ourselves*, or still more correctly, the immediate knowledge which we have of each of the facts which occur in our sensibility, in our intelligence, and in our will.

89. Characteristics of Consciousness. — Consciousness is a *perception*, or rather an intuition, that is to say, it is knowledge immediate and native.

To perceive is to know a particular object without intervention, at the first glance. We perceive a pain, a sound, a savor. Consciousness is inward perception ; the senses are the organs of outward perception.

90. Perceiving and Conceiving. — In philosophical language, *perception* is sharply distinguished from *conception*.

Conception is a derivative, secondary operation of the intelligence. Through imagination we conceive a vast edifice, or the entire world. Through abstraction we conceive numbers, and through generalization, humanity. Conception, moreover, does not necessarily involve a belief in the existence of the object conceived ; it is not fatally bound up in a judgment. We can conceive a fine summer for the approaching season without believing in it ; we can conceive humanity without affirming anything of it for the moment.

Perception, on the contrary, always gives rise to a judgment. My consciousness, my senses, never present to me isolated ideas, but always affirmations based at least on the existence of the object perceived.

91. Degrees of Consciousness. — Psychological phenomena in general, and those of consciousness in particular, are not absolute and invariable states. If they could be measured, it would be seen that they pass through very different stages, from a minimum almost equal to zero, up to a very high maximum.

There are moments when a full light breaks in upon our minds ; we see with perfect clearness the least particulars, the smallest details, of the thought present to our intelligence ; it is the broad daylight of consciousness.

But in other cases, on the contrary, we discern with difficulty, confusedly and obscurely, the object of our thought ; it is the half glimmer of the twilight, which indeed scatters the shadows of the night, but does not wholly light us.

" Psychological facts are susceptible of an infinite number of degrees, and, like them and with them, consciousness may decrease indefinitely without ceasing to be. There are atoms of consciousness in the world of the soul, just as there are atoms of matter in the physical world." [1]

92. Causes of the Variations in the Intensity of Consciousness. — The degree of consciousness depends in

[1] Rabier, *op. cit.*, p. 54.

part upon the nature of the phenomena of which we take knowledge. The facts which have for immediate antecedents certain organic phenomena, as the appetites, for example, are scarcely conscious. On the contrary, the facts of moral sensibility, of abstract intelligence, and of will, which depend only very indirectly on physiological functions, acquire a full consciousness of themselves. In other terms, in proportion as the facts become more psychological, the consciousness gains in power and clearness. In fact, consciousness is the very essence of psychological phenomena. It is not, properly speaking, a distinct faculty, but is the succession of moral facts which come to a knowledge of themselves as they are severally produced.

Consequently, the degree of consciousness depends on all the causes which diminish or increase the intensity of psychological activity. Thus, in the first moments following our awakening, we have but a vague consciousness of ourselves; our dreams are still prolonged, and, the psychological life not having yet regained its entire lucidity, the consciousness feels the effect of it.

Consciousness, in a word, is to the mind what light is to the flame. The more combustion increases, the more intense the flame and the more vivid and brilliant the light.

93. Spontaneous Consciousness and Reflective Consciousness. — What we have just said is true only of the

spontaneous consciousness which accompanies psychological phenomena without effort. But the attention
exercises its authority over consciousness, as over the
other intellectual operations; and consciousness then
becomes reflection, that is, attention brought to bear on
the phenomena of spirit.

In this case the mind divides itself into two, so to
speak; the thinking subject becomes the object of
thought, and through the attention, which is an effort
or act of the will, we no longer simply see ourselves,
but we observe ourselves. And this attentive notice
doubles or triples the scope of vision; to look atten-
tively is to see with a magnifying glass or with a lens.
This attentive consciousness, it has very often been
said, is not in accord with the natural tendencies of the
mind. We are but little inclined to throw ourselves
back upon ourselves, hurried on as we are to observe
what is about us. But a little effort and some experience suffice to render this inward observation as familiar to us as outward observation. Psychologists and
men of meditative disposition easily become capable of
this self-observation, and of practising this art of reflection which is the principle or basis of all psychological
science.

94. Are There Unconscious Phenomena? — Beyond
and around the sphere which consciousness illumines,
is there a zone of unconscious phenomena which ought,
nevertheless, to be considered as psychological phenom-

ena ? Without making an abuse of the unconscious, as certain contemporary philosophers have done, Hartmann,* for example, it is impossible not to recognize around this luminous centre called consciousness, a twilight border which even extends into the shadows of the unconscious.

Leibnitz long ago called attention to the fact that we are not always conscious of certain obscure, unobserved perceptions, so feeble that they are not observed in their passage, but which nevertheless leave a trace in our minds. Of this class, for example, is the noise of the mill which the sleepy miller does not seem to hear, but which nevertheless he does hear in a certain measure, for if the noise ceases the miller awakes. The same is true of the tiresome sermon whose monotonous delivery puts the hearer to sleep, but who awakes when the sermon is finished ; and of this class are the various impressions which the senses transmit to us while we read or meditate, indifferent to all that is transpiring around us, and of which we take no account till we are aroused from our reverie. It is well known that under the influence of fever or nervous agitation, invalids have been known to speak a language which they were not at all accustomed to use ; as, for example, the servant of Coleridge,* who spoke Hebrew while in a paroxysm of fever, because in her youth she had heard her master read aloud from his Hebrew Bible. Without suspecting it, the sounds of the unknown tongue were engraven on her memory.

But these obscure perceptions are not properly speaking unconscious facts, but are facts of lesser or intermittent consciousness ; and, in fact, the mind, not being able to think of more than one thing at a time, [1] is ever passing from unconsciousness to consciousness.

95. Knowledge which we owe to Consciousness. — As consciousness accompanies all psychological facts, it is to it that we owe the knowledge of all intellectual and moral facts.

We have no idea of remorse except as we have experienced it ; we do not attach a definite meaning to the words joy, sadness, ambition, and friendship, except as we have been conscious of these feelings.

There are men whose consciousness is partly blind and deaf, just as, with respect to external perception, there are men who neither see nor hear ; because their minds are incomplete, inaccessible to certain psychological phenomena.

96. The Idea of Self. — The consciousness is an uninterrupted procession of individual perceptions ; but we connect with ourselves all these perceptions which drop into our thought, one by one. The consciousness, aided by the other operations of the mind, furnishes us with the idea of self.

This idea is not one of those which the child acquires immediately. It presupposes some effort at reflection and some comparison between the successive perceptions of the consciousness.

---

[1] For a different view, see Hamilton, *Metaphysics*, p. 165.

"By a process of abstraction similar to that whereby the child learns to group external objects according to their resemblances, he comes to a knowledge of the inner and moral world, his own mind and character. His idea of self begins with the perception of his own organism, as the object in which he localizes his various feelings of pleasure and pain. Even this partial idea is slowly acquired. As Professor Preyer points out, the infant does not at first know his own organism as something related to his feelings of pleasure and pain. When more than a year old, his boy bit his own arm just as though it had been a foreign object. This crude and material form of self-consciousness seems to correspond to the early period of life, in which the child speaks of himself by his proper name.

"As the power of abstraction grows, this idea of self becomes fuller, and includes the representation of internal mental states. The child's attention is absorbed in outward things. To attend to the facts of the inner life implies an effort, an active withdrawal of the mind from the outer world. More particularly its development would be promoted by the experience of moral discipline and the reception of blame or praise. It is when the child's attention is driven inward, in an act of reflection on his own actions as springing from good or bad motives, that he wakes up to a fuller consciousness of self.

"The gradual substitution for the proper name of

'me,' ' I,' 'my,' which is observable in the third year, probably marks the date of more distinct reflection on internal feelings, and consequently of a clearer idea of self as a conscious moral being.

"A further process of abstraction is implied in arriving at the idea of a *permanent* self. The assurance of an enduring mental self, one and the same through all the changes of feeling, involves a certain development of the child's memory." [1]

Omitting what the idea of self may owe to the sense-perception of our body, this idea results chiefly from the comparison which the mind makes between its different states of consciousness. Notwithstanding their diversity, they all have something in common, and this common quality is, that they are recognized as *ours*. By means of the memory, and through the process of abstraction which detects in the various phenomena their common quality of being conscious in the same manner, we rise without difficulty to the idea of our own personal existence.

97. The Idea of Substance and the Idea of Cause. — The idea of a permanent self is the basis or material, so to speak, of the general idea of substance which has played such an important part in the history of philosophy.

Substance is precisely something which remains the same, which endures through apparent modifications and perpetual changes.

---

[1] Sully's *Hand-Book of Psychology*, p. 211.

Permanence in the form of sensible objects may doubtless contribute towards causing us to acquire the idea of an invariable substance; but it is only in ourselves, through the consciousness of our personal identity, that we reach an experimental knowledge of substance, that is, of a permanent being. [1]

In the same way, consciousness is the source of the notion of cause, that is, of the relation which exists between an acting force and resulting effect. In the external world we grasp phenomena which follow one another in constant succession. But the relation of "causality" is something more than the idea of an invariable succession; it is the idea of an efficient activity, of an effort followed by an effect; it is within ourselves, in the consciousness of our activity directed towards an end and tending to an act which it foresees and produces, that we grasp for the first time, in the very act, an efficient cause. This notion of cause, derived at first from our own experience, we then generalize and transfer to the external world.

98. Attention. — It is not to spontaneous consciousness reduced to itself, but to consciousness prolonged by the memory and aided by reflective comparison, — in a word, it is to *attention*, that we owe the knowledge of which mention has just been made.

---

[1] " The idea of substance may be derived from the idea of self. The Ego appears to itself as something individual, as something identical. It may, then, better than external objects, furnish the intelligence with the type from which is derived the notion of substance." (Rabier, *op. cit.*, p. 289.)

Attention is not a special intellectual function ; it is a general and voluntary mode of the intelligence. It is *the* intelligence disciplined by the will. It may be defined as *the self-governing intelligence applying itself to what it wills.*

By this definition we exclude from the domain of attention states of consciousness which resemble it ; for example, states in which the intelligence is absorbed by an impression which dominates and subjects it. A dominant, exclusive perception cannot be confounded with real attention, which is precisely the power of escaping from the yoke of the sensations, and of directing itself voluntarily towards the objects which we have chosen. In a word, attention is the liberty of the mind.

99. Attention, the Instrument of Education — Attention is the condition of the development of all the intellectual faculties. We shall find it, active and efficient, in all the operations of the mind, assuring to each of them its maximum of energy. It is pre-eminently a pedagogical faculty, that is, an instrument of education. This is why, in our *Lectures on Pedagogy,*[1] we have discussed at length its importance, its beginning and progress, its characteristics and conditions. It is useless to return to a theory which pertains to the art of education rather than to psychology proper. It suffices to have indicated the place of attention and to have given a succinct exposition of its laws.

100 Laws of Attention. — I. Attention is doubtless

[1] See Compayré's *Lectures on Pedagogy,* Boston, 1888, ch. v.

the result of an effort of the mind and of an application : of the will. But, no mental act being absolutely independent and self-existent, this effort in turn depends in part upon the intelligence and the sensibility. Our will summons to itself all the energies of the mind to no purpose, if the object which it proposes to our attention does not respond to our capacities and intellectual habits ; it will not succeed at all, or will succeed but poorly, in fixing our meditations. So, also, it is useful, as aiding the task of attention, that the object studied should be attractive to us and that our feelings should find their gratification in it. In other terms, everything in our moral life is coherent and connected ; and if the attention is the application of the will to the intelligence, the will, in order to apply itself, has need that the intelligence and the sensibility lend it their assistance.

2. The attention has a double result : (*a*) To circumscribe the object to be known, to define the exact limits of the field of our mental effort, and to reduce its extent. By this means it divides the difficulties in order the better to resolve them.

(*b*) On the other hand, it concentrates the intellectual powers on a given point ; and, instead of allowing them to be scattered in different directions, it vigorously brings them to bear on a given purpose.

These two reasons suffice to explain the results of attention and the happy influence which it exercises on intellectual labor.

101. Attention, Comparison, Reflection. — Psychological language, a little too copious to be wholly precise, employs several expressions to designate different shades of attention.

On the authority of some philosophers, the word *attention* should be reserved for the application of the mind to what is external to us. *Reflection*, on the contrary, would be attention to what is within. We shall not oppose this view, although it seems preferable to preserve to attention its more general signification, and to attribute to it all the efforts of thought, whatever may be its object. On the other hand, *comparison* is also a form of attention ; it is attention directed to two ideas or two objects, — as it were, a double attention, tending to grasp the relations of things.

But under all its forms attention always remains the reflective mode of the intelligence, the real "might of the spirit," to use the expression of Malebranche : * and, as he says again in his picturesque language, "the prayer which we address to Truth in order that she may become ours."

SUMMARY.

42. CONSCIOUSNESS is the general form of all the intellectual facts. The **ATTENTION** is one of its essential modes, the voluntary mode.

43. Consciousness is the knowledge which we have of all sensitive, intellectual, and voluntary facts.

44. CONSCIOUSNESS IS A PERCEPTION. PERCEP-TION is immediate, primitive knowledge, always accompanied by judgment. **CONCEPTION** is a derived knowledge, which does not always give rise to a judgment.

45. Consciousness is **INWARD PERCEPTION,** an **INTERNAL SENSE.** The five senses proper are the organs of **EXTERNAL PERCEPTION.**

46. Consciousness is susceptible of a great number of degrees. Its power is always measured by the degree of strength attained by the different psychological functions.

47. The power of consciousness depends also on effort, on the voluntary application which transforms **SPONTANEOUS** consciousness into **REFLECTIVE** consciousness.

48. There are unobserved perceptions which suppose a lower degree of consciousness and are almost unconscious.

49. Consciousness makes us acquainted, in the first place, with all the moral and intellectual phenomena which take place within us.

50. It is consciousness, also, which connects all these phenomena with a principle, one and identical, the subject of all these phenomena, the **EGO.**

51. By this means, again, consciousness presents to us the primary type of **SUBSTANCE** and **CAUSALITY.**

52. ATTENTION is the reflective or voluntary form of all intellectual facts.

53. Although it is an act of the will, attention itself depends on the intelligence and the sensibility.

CHAPTER VI

OUTWARD PERCEPTION. THE FIVE SENSES

102. Definition of Outward Perception. — Outward perception is the intellectual function through which we gain an immediate knowledge of the qualities of the external world.

The instruments of outward perception are the material organs located in different parts of the body and called the organs of sense.

103. The Five Senses. — The senses are five in number: smell, taste, hearing, sight, and touch. Some philosophers, and particularly the English psychologists, assert that it would be better to include two more, — the muscular sense and the general organic sense. " By this expression (muscular sense) is meant the sum of those peculiar 'sensations' of which we are aware when we voluntary exercise our muscles. The sensations which accompany muscular action may be conveniently divided into two main varieties. These are (*a*) sensations of movement or of unimpeded energy, and (*b*) sensations of strain or resistance, that is, of obstructed or impeded energy." [1]

But, in reality, these muscular sensations are scarcely

---

[1] Sully's *Teacher's Hand-Book of Psychology*, p. 93.

perceptions ; they teach us nothing of matter, except that it resists us, and impedes our liberty of movement ; they consist chiefly in an impression of agreeable activity or of painful effort.

This is still more true of the general organic sense, which Mr. Sully defines as follows :

" The sensations falling under the head of common sensibility, or of the organic sense, are marked by the absence of definite characters. They are vague and ill-defined. Their distinguishing peculiarity is that they have a marked pleasurable or painful aspect. Such are the feelings of comfort and discomfort connected with the processes of digestion and indigestion, and with injuries to the tissues. These sensations are not directly connected with the action of external objects, but arise in consequence of a certain condition of the part of the organism concerned. Thus they give us no knowledge of the external world." [1]

We can then hold to the old classical distinction of the five senses, because they alone furnish us with definite notions as to the qualities of matter.

104. Sensations and Perceptions. — As we have already seen (Chapter III.) the five senses are at the same time the seat of affective phenomena and of representative phenomena, — of sensations and perceptions.

At first, it is the affective element which dominates ; it is pleasure or pain which constitutes the " whole " of

---

[1] Sully's *Teacher's Hand-Book of Psychology*, p. 87.

sensation. But little by little the representative element disengages itself, and perception appears. This
is what Hamilton [1] expressed by saying : " Knowledge
and feeling, — perception and sensation, though always
co-existent, are always in the inverse ratio of each
other."

Doubtless, for the child the sensations of sight are
intense pleasures which vividly excite his sensibility,
but which bring him only vague representations of the
external world. On the contrary, in the mature man,
it is only exceptionally that the perceptions of sight are
accompanied by pleasure or by pain.

105. The Subjective and the Objective. — This is the
proper place to indicate an essential distinction of
which philosophers make a great use, — between the
subjective and the *objective*. A sensation is merely subjective ; in other terms, it is an inward phenomenon
which is related only to the feeling subject. A perception, on the contrary, is objective, it represents to us
an object distinct from the subject.

106. Hierarchy of the Five Senses. — The five senses
are far from being equally important with respect to
perceptions and the objective representations of which
they are the source.

In the impressions of taste and smell, pains and
pleasures dominate ; servants of the sensibility, these
two senses are but indifferent instruments of the intel-

[1] Hamilton, *Metaphysics*, p. 336.

ligence. Hearing, sight, and touch, on the contrary, furnish us with perceptions which are usually indifferent, that is, divorced from all emotion, agreeable or disagreeable, but which constitute real intellectual knowledge.

107. Micromégas* and the Plurality of the Senses. — The five senses reveal to us very many of the properties of matter; but it is evident that they do not reveal to us all of them; and that an additional sense, if it existed, would give us the knowledge of new qualities. In one of his most ingenious romances, Voltaire imagines a giant, who, endowed with more senses than man has, distinguishes in matter a multitude of properties which are unknown to us.

" How many senses do the men of your globe have? asks the inhabitant of Sirius of the inhabitant of Saturn. We have sixty-two, says the Saturnian, and every day we complain of the small number. I can well believe it, says Micromégas, for in our globe we have nearly a thousand senses, and we ever feel a vague longing which suggests to us that there are beings much more perfect than we are. How many different properties do you count in the matter of your world? — If you speak of those properties without which we believe this globe could not remain as it is, we count three hundred, extension, impenetrability, mobility, divisibility, and the rest." [1]

108. Analysis of Sense Perception. — Though exter-

---

[1] Micromégas. *Histoire philosophique.*

nal perception furnishes an immediate knowledge of material reality, it is nevertheless a complex operation involving many others. It first supposes the existence of an external phenomenon, of a physical object or a material quality, which is the cause of the perception. It then necessitates a series of physiological phenomena which take place : (1) in the external organ placed on the surface of the body where the impression is produced ; (2) in the special nerves, — the optic nerves for seeing, the acoustic nerves for hearing, etc., which transmit to the nerve centre the impression received from without ; (3) in the brain, where, following the transmitted impression, the perception takes place.

Perception is thus a psychological phenomenon which involves, as antecedents, physical and physiological phenomena.

109. A General Description of the Apparatus of Sensation. — Let us take the sense of sight, as an example. In darkness we see nothing, nor do we see anything more in a vacuum. In order that perception of sight may take place, light must illumine us and also the object placed before us. In the second place, there must be an organ of vision and it must be sound. The eye is like a window opened to the external world. If the window is closed or in any way obstructed, the light does not penetrate the house, or penetrates it imperfectly. But this is not all. If the optic nerve placed behind the retina which carpets the back of the eye is cut or destroyed, the luminous ray will strike the eye to no purpose. Not having been transmitted to the brain, it will not be perceived.

Without entering into details which fall within the province of physiology, we conclude that the organs of sense are a special apparatus giving rise to particular perceptions. The sense of touch alone is distributed over the whole surface of the body, although its principal seat is in the hand.

110. Perceptions, Natural and Acquired. — There is an essential distinction which should be understood from the very first. Among the perceptions, some result immediately from the natural play of each sense ; these are *natural perceptions*. Others suppose a certain education of the senses and their mutual co-operation ; these are *acquired perceptions*. Thus, we shall presently see that color is a natural perception of sight, and the distance of objects an acquired perception.

111. Perceptions, Passive and Active. — Another important distinction is that between spontaneous or passive perceptions, and perceptions that are voluntary or active. The attention plays an important part in external perception as in other functions of the mind. It is one thing to observe, to listen, to feel, to discriminate by taste and smell ; and another to see, to hear, to touch, and simply to taste and smell. Perception attains its maximum of power only when it is directed by the attention.

Each of our senses procures for us special perceptions, absolutely irreducible to any others. Let us
study these specific perceptions in order.

112. Perceptions of Smell and Taste. — The special
perceptions of smell and taste are *odors* and *savors*.

Smell and taste are two inferior senses which bring
us more sensations than perceptions, to which we owe
more pleasures than ideas. Odors and savors, as we
have said, are impressions, agreeable or disagreeable,
according to circumstances, rather than intellectual
phenomena, knowledges, or representative facts.

Nevertheless, odors and savors, being distinct qualities of matter, may aid us in recognizing bodies.
Chemists, in their analyses and classifications, use the
characteristic odors of different substances in order to
distinguish them one from another. And so the wine-
taster learns to distinguish the vintage of a wine by its
particular taste. Each one of us has need of the sense
of taste in order to distinguish foods, and to avoid de-
ception in them.

113. Perceptions of Hearing. — The special perception
of hearing is *sound* and its different qualities.

The different characteristics of sound may be classed
as follows : (1) quality, the sound is sweet or harsh ;
(2) intensity, the sound is strong or weak ; (3) volume,
which depends on the extent of the sonorous mass ; (4)
pitch, the sound is shrill or grave ; (5) timbre, which
comes from the difference in voices or instruments.

Hearing is a social sense, for it is through it that we perceive the language of our fellows, and language is one of the foundations of society.

It is a musical sense, for it is through the perception of differences in the pitch of sounds that we are sensible of the charm of music.

Besides, through education and the co-operation of other senses, hearing acquires the perception of distance and the direction of sounds. Accustomed as we are by experience to associate sounds with the presence of a given object, we come to judge from the sound alone, from its nature and intensity, whether the object which produces it is far away or near at hand. A feeble sound is a sign that the object is remote, and *vice versa*.

114. Perceptions of Sight. — The proper and natural perception of sight is *color*, but color being always united with surface, surface is also the immediate object of the perception of sight.

It must be added, it is true, that the eyes never really perceive extension unless they can move. We move them to the right and left and thus extend the field of vision. (See Compayré's *Lectures on Pedagogy*.) But if the sight naturally perceives extension in its two primary dimensions, length and breadth ; and if, through the differences of color which mark and limit it, it immediately grasps the form of objects ; the same thing is not true in respect of the third dimension of bodies, depth or thickness, and, consequently, with respect to the distance of objects.

Depth and distance are not natural data, but are acquired perceptions of sight.

To prove this, it suffices to recollect that the child is for a long time very awkward in his appreciation of distances; he stretches out his hand to grasp objects which are wholly beyond his reach.   ·

Moreover, numerous experiments made on persons blind from birth allow no doubt on this question.

115. Cheselden's Experiment. — Cheselden,* a surgeon of the eighteenth century, having cured a blind man of cataract, ascertained that the patient, at the moment when he recovered his sight, had no perception of distance or of solidity ; the objects which he saw presented themselves to him on the same plane, glued, so to speak, to the same surface ; they touched his eyes.   He confounded a flat disk with a globe, and touch alone taught him to recognize the difference between a plane surface and solid bodies.

This experiment has often been repeated, and always with the same results.[1]

116. Perception of Solidity. — It follows that the perception of depth and distance is due to a co-operation of eye and hand, and that it supposes even the intervention of reasoning and of a rapid induction.   Sight allows us to perceive different degrees of light, degradations and shadows.   Touch, on the other hand,

---

[1] See Taine, *On Intelligence*, vol. l.

teaches us, through the resistance which bodies offer to it, the difference between a plane surface over which our figures slide, and a solid body which our hand passes around. We very soon learn to associate these two sorts of perceptions and to note what play of light and shade corresponds to a simple surface, and what to a solid body ; so that by the sight of an object, according as it is illuminated one way or another, we judge of its three dimensions.

And so for distance. Experience has taught us that objects appear smaller to us in proportion as they are more remote, and larger as they are nearer us ; so that we judge from their apparent size of the distance which separates them from us. The acquired perceptions of a sense are, then, at bottom, natural perceptions interpreted by the reason through experience and the aid of the other senses.

The natural perceptions of the senses are infallible as long as the senses remain in their normal state ; but the acquired perceptions, being the result of a rational interpretation of natural perceptions, are subject to error.

We are often deceived in our estimate of the thickness and distance of objects. A false window, simply represented upon a wall, gives us the illusion of a real window. The painter who skilfully arranges colors, lights, and shades on his canvas, makes us believe in the existence of several planes on the same surface.

All the illusions of perspective are based on the psychological fact that the perception of depth and distance is an acquired perception.

117. Perceptions of Touch. — The perceptions of touch are quite numerous : they are, first the rough and the smooth, then the hot and the cold, and lastly and chiefly, resistance and solidity.

Touch, it has been said, is the true sense of exteriority ; that which reveals to us, without possible dispute, the existence of something exterior which resists our pressure and which, consequently, is distinct from us.

118. Laura Bridgman. — Touch has this special characteristic, that being distributed over the whole surface of the body, it is never completely abolished.

There are mutes and persons blind from birth or by accident, but there is no living creature deprived of the sense of touch ; and through this sense there have been exceptional cases, like that of Laura Bridgman, of persons deprived of sight and hearing, who have been able to read and write, and through signs to hold communication with other persons. Laura Bridgman, a deaf mute and blind from birth, was able to sew and embroider ; she distinguished the color of the silk or cotton which she used ; she wrote verse ; and through a remarkable substitution of the sense of touch, cultivated and prodigiously developed, for the senses which she lacked, she finally became an intelligent, well-informed, and relatively happy person.

119. Errors of the Senses. — Much has been said of the errors of the senses. Those of vision have often been cited, as the illusion of the stick which seems broken when one end is plunged in water, or of the square tower which at a distance seems round. In truth, these errors are to be attributed, not to the senses themselves, but to the reason, which wrongly interprets the appearances of sense, or which, withdrawing a sense from the limits of its special competence, demands of it information which only another sense can supply. The appearances of sense are always what they ought to be. For example, by the laws of refraction of light, the physicist explains the phenomenon of the stick which seems broken. But by reason of the habit which we have formed of associating a judgment as to the real conditions of bodies with the colored appearances of these same bodies, we are the dupes, in certain cases, of these same appearances; we are deceived when, for one reason or another, they do not coincide with the reality.

120. Hallucination. — In reality, the sole error of the senses is hallucination. In this case we believe we see and hear, when in reality there is no visible object, no sonorous body, within the reach of these senses. Hallucination is a false, a purely subjective perception, which corresponds to no objective reality.

And it is easy, moreover, to explain this error, or rather this disease of the senses. In the normal state, perception is the consequence of a series of nervous phenomena determined by the external impression of a real object. But in certain abnormal states, the nervous excitation may be the result of the imagination, an organic disorder. The optic nerve then vibrates as if it were affected by a luminous object; and the mind projects outwardly, as though it corresponded to a reality, the image which is transmitted to it, but which is only a phantom.

121. Relativity of Sense-Knowledge. — If there is one truth that is well established in philosophy, it is that sense-knowledge is relative; it is derived from the relation of two terms, the exterior object and the organization of our senses. Modify the sensitive apparatus, and the perception will vary. It is in this way that the eye, when affected by jaundice, sees everything in yellow; and that through the infirmity called " Daltonism," * the eye is incapable of distinguishing red.

That which is too heavy for the frail hand of a child is not so for the robust hand of a grown man. The senses do not give us absolute knowledge.[1] What seems small to the natural eye seems large when seen with the microscope.

On the other hand, it is very evident that sense-per-

[1] According to certain philosophers, it is necessary to distinguish the *primary qualities* of matter, such as extension, divisibility, form, etc.; and *secondary qualities*, such as taste, color, smell, etc. The first alone are absolute knowledges. Modern philosophers have no difficulty in showing that extension itself is a relative knowledge, for it varies with the visual organ.

ceptions do not resemble the material phenomena which produce them. They are signs which in their own way translate the thing signified.

Outside of ourselves, sound, as we know, is but a movement of matter ; and light is also but a movement. We should be well convinced of this truth, that if there were no ear there would be no sounds ; and if there were no eyes there would no longer be light in nature. Matter, so to speak, is, in itself, an inaccessible and illegible text which we know only through a translation.

122. Idealism. — From the relativity of sense-knowledge, certain philosophers have drawn the extreme and unwarrantable conclusion that the external world is an illusion, a vain appearance. Berkeley* maintained that matter does not exist, and that all reality is reducible to our states of consciousness. This is the doctrine called idealism.*

123. Reality of the External World. — It must be said in reply to Berkeley, that if the senses do not give us an adequate knowledge of matter, if they do not teach us what the external world is in itself, they do, at least, reveal to us that there is something outside of ourselves, and that there is an external world.

If there were only the perceptions of hearing, smell, and taste, they might be considered, up to a certain point, as purely subjective impressions which, through illusion, we project outwardly by referring them to an imaginary substance.

But how can we persist in this opinion in the presence of the perception of visual extension, so radically opposed to our states of unextended consciousness, and especially in the presence of tactile impressions and of the resistance opposed to touch by that unknown something which is outside of ourselves? If Descartes could say : "I think, therefore I am ;" it is permissible to add, by an analogous formula : "I feel, I touch something which resists, I perceive something extended ; therefore there is something outside of myself."

Let us add, moreover, that belief in the external world, or the idea of matter distinct from ourselves, is not an immediate perception of the senses, the result of a direct experience ; but is a derived conception which is organized in the mind little by little. The senses reveal to us immediately only particular qualities, and it is only through the association and co-ordination of their different impressions, united insensibly into one single and unique picture, that we come to *objectify*,* or to project outwardly, and to consider as a distinct substance, the cause of all these sense-perceptions.

SUMMARY.

54. OUTWARD PERCEPTION is the intellectual function by which we take immediate knowledge of the external world.

-**55.** The organs of outward perception are the five senses : **SMELL, TASTE, HEARING, SEEING** and **TOUCH.** Some

\

psychologists also distinguish the muscular sense and the general organic sense.

56. THE SENSATIONS are affective phenomena of pleasure or pain; THE PERCEPTIONS are representative phenomena. It may be said, farther, that sensation is SUBJECTIVE, and perception OBJECTIVE.

57. The senses may be classed in the following order with respect to the services which they render the intelligence : 1, seeing ; 2, hearing ; 3, touch ; 4, smell ; 5. taste.

58. Outward perception is a psychological phenomenon, which supposes a PHYSICAL PHENOMENON, namely, the object of perception ; and certain PHYSIOLOGICAL CONDITIONS, as the outward organ of the senses, the nerves, and the brain.

59. Each of the senses furnishes us with special perceptions, some of them NATURAL and others ACQUIRED, some PASSIVE and others ACTIVE.

60. The proper perceptions of SMELL and TASTE are ODORS and SAVORS.

61. The proper perceptions of HEARING are sound and its different qualities. The ear perceives the direction and distance of sounds only through the aid of experience and reasoning.

62. The natural perceptions of SIGHT are COLOR and EXTENT of surface. The perception of DISTANCE and SOLIDITY is an ACQUIRED PERCEPTION of sight.

63. The principal perception of TOUCH is SOLIDITY or RESISTANCE.

64. The senses are infallible when they do not go out of their proper domain.

65. HALLUCINATION is a false perception.

66. Sense-knowledge is relative ; but if it does not make us know matter in itself, it nevertheless reveals to us in a **CERTAIN MANNER** the existence of matter.

CHAPTER VII

ANALYSIS AND EXPLANATION OF THE PHENOMENA OF MEMORY

124. Memory the Function of Conservation. — The intellectual faculties of which we have been speaking, are functions of acquisition. Consciousness reveals to us immediately the world within ; and the senses, the world without. But these gifts of consciousness would be but a useless succession of transient and perishable phenomena, an accumulation of the facts of consciousness disappearing as soon as they had appeared, if they had not been preserved by the memory. Without the memory the mind would be like the cask of the Danaides,* emptying itself while being filled. In truth, the mind would not exist ; for the intelligence supposes not only the incessant and ever-continued acquisition of new knowledge ; but in order to exist, it must have the power to hold what it acquires, and always to have at its disposal the elementary knowledge which is the material of subsequent knowledge.[1]

Let us add that the memory preserves and renews,

---

[1] Some psychologists, notably F. Marion, place the study of the functions of conservation after the study of the functions of elaboration. We believe that it is more logical, when we have examined the primitive faculties of perception, to pass at once to the memory, which is the condition of the subsequent activity of the mind.

not only the knowledge that has been acquired by the senses and the consciousness, but also the knowledge derived from the faculties of elaboration.

125. Memory and Consciousness. — Under whatever form the memory presents itself, the facts which ought to be assigned to it are always recollections or impressions remaining in the memory; and recollections are derived, or secondary, states of consciousness, as distinguished from perceptions, which constitute the primitive facts of the mind.

There is nothing, there can be nothing, in the memory, which has not previously been in the consciousness.

Conversely, whatever has been, at a given moment, a fact of consciousness, may become, at a subsequent moment, a fact of memory.

We recall sounds, colors and forms, savors and odors, and tactile impressions; and we also recall the emotions, agreeable or disagreeable, which have traversed our sensibility. " Properly speaking," says Royer-Collard,* " we recollect only the operations and different states of our mind, because we recollect nothing that has not been the immediate intuition of our consciousness. This assertion seems to contradict common sense, according to which we do not hesitate to say, *I remember such a person ;* but the contradiction is only apparent. *I remember such a person* means, *I remember to have seen such a person."* [1]

<hr>

[1] *Fragments de Royer-Collard*, p. 357.

But if the reviving power of the memory cannot in any case go beyond the compass of the acquisitions of consciousness, the converse is far from being absolutely true, that every primitive state of consciousness remains fixed in the memory. By the side of memory there is forgetfulness; not only the temporary forgetfulness into which all our knowledge falls the moment we no longer think of it; but also the final forgetfulness to which are condemned a multitude of the states of consciousness which will no more reappear, either because the occasion favorable for their reappearance will not occur, or because the powers of the memory are unable to retain all that has successively passed before our consciousness.

In fact, then, memory is but a partial restoration of thoughts previously acquired.

126. Definition of Memory. — For the present, memory may be defined as the *intellectual function which preserves and renews inner states of consciousness.* It does not comprise merely the facts of actual remembrance, but also the latent disposition that makes it possible for these remembrances to reappear at some future time.

It is then an inexact definition of memory to say with Reid,* that it is "the immediate knowledge of the past." First, "immediate knowledge" is inexact, since memory is a derived fact, subsequent to an original perception. Next, and chiefly, memory is not merely the intermittent succession of conscious and actual recollections ; but it is also the possibility of recollecting, a possibility that may never be realized. It is the sum of the aptitudes which we acquire to represent to ourselves a second time that which has once been present to our minds.

127. Importance of the Memory. — It is useless to insist on a truth so elementary as the importance of the memory. Without the memory, no intellectual operation is possible. When the perceptions have lasted a certain length of time, it is assumed that at the moment when they cease we have not forgotten the first impressions which they gave us at the outset. Reasoning, which always comprises a series of judgments, requires that the mind, when it reaches the conclusion, should recall the premises on which it is founded. And if, under its humbler form and in its ordinary proportions, memory is one of the necessary conditions of all the operations of the mind, it becomes, when it is particularly strong and well developed, one of the sources of the power and wealth of the intellect ; for it is the memory which enriches and supplies it more or less with its stores.

128. Analysis of the Facts of Memory. — There are several periods to distinguish in the phenomena of memory. At first, memory is but the prolongation in consciousness of a received impression which continues, and, so to speak, resounds for a little after the instant

when it was produced. Thus, for a long time after it
has tolled, we continue to hear the bell which strikes
our ears. We have opened our eyes to view a landscape ; we close them ; and we still see with our mind's
eye the different objects which we have perceived. In
this case memory is nothing but a prolonged consciousness ; no interval separates the original perception and
the recollection which we preserve of it. In most cases,
on the contrary, recollection is preceded by forgetfulness. During our lives we have perceived a multitude
of objects ; we have acquired a mass of knowledge.
All this knowledge, all these perceptions, remain dormant, so to speak, in our intelligence ; but we have the
faculty of awakening them, and it is precisely in this
that memory consists. True memory is the resurrec-
tion or reappearance in the consciousness of knowledge
for a time forgotten, but which revives after a longer or
shorter period of unconsciousness and forgetfulness.

129. Reminiscence and Recognition. — But this reappearance or restoration of knowledge does not always
take place in the same manner ; and there is a distinction to be made between *reminiscence*, which is but an
incomplete or half recollection, and *recognition*, which
is the integral form of the memory. It often happens
that a representation reappears in our mind without our
being able to say when and how it appeared there for
the first time, and even without our knowing that
it is the renewal of an earlier state of consciousness.

In this case the phenomenon of memory is a simple reminiscence. But still oftener the representations of the memory are, as Locke * says, accompanied by an additional perception indicating that they are not new, that they have already been experienced; this is what is ordinarily called recognition. In fact, true memory consists in recognizing, or replacing in the past, the representation which returns to our mind. Recollection will be the clearer and the more definite as we are the better able to refer it, in time and space, to the place and the moment when it was engraven in our memory.

130. Explanation of Memory. — Philosophers have multiplied their theories to explain the phenomena of memory; but perhaps it must be acknowledged that these explanations do not lead to a clear solution, and that the memory is an irreducible fact which defies analysis.

According to certain philosophers, recollections remain in the mind as precious objects remain in the casket or dark drawer where they have been shut up, till the day when they have been restored to the light. For acquired knowledge there is a sort of unconscious survival. The mind, according to Plato, is a dove-cote full of birds that are waiting till some one comes to take them and restore them to the broad day-light. In other terms, our conscious perceptions subsist in the state of insensible and unconscious thought.

This hypothesis cannot be admitted; for we cannot

conceive of unconscious thoughts. There is an absolute contradiction in conceiving a thought which is not thought. Acquired knowledge, the moment it is no longer present to the mind, evidently no longer exists in the state of knowledge.

The essence of psychological facts is that they are conscious ; suppress consciousness and they will cease to exist.

131. Physiological Explanation. — A more plausible theory for explaining the latent persistence and intermittent reappearance of recollections, assumes that there subsist in the brain organic traces or material imprints corresponding to each item of acquired knowledge. The old comparison, which likened the memory to a treasury or a storehouse, is, by this theory, amply justified. The brain contains, in the state of real traces or of infinitely small characters, all the recollections which throng the memory. It is in this sense that Descartes compared the mind, with respect to its power of recollection, to a sheet of paper, or to a piece of canvas, which, once bent in a certain way, indefinitely preserves the fold which has been given it, and which it tends to take again.

It may be objected, it is true, that the recollections which the mind holds in store are innumerable, and that it is difficult to conceive the material possibility of lodging in the brain the enormous quantity of distinct and individual traces which this accumulation of dormant knowledge supposes. Philosophers reply to this objection by saying that the complexity of nervous matter is infinite; that the brain contains six hundred millions of cells and several thousand millions of fibres.

But this physiological explanation does not solve all the difficulties in the case. We are quite willing to admit that the memory has its conditions in the brain; but we are at a loss to understand how these material traces imprinted in the nervous substance, just as letters are stamped on a sheet of white paper, do not always remain present to consciousness; but that at one time they remain concealed, ignored by the mind which possesses them, while at another they revive and reappear under the eye of consciousness.

132. Memory is a Habit. — Here the psychologists interpose, who define memory as an *intellectual habit*, a permanent disposition of the mind to think anew what it has already thought.

But this apparent explanation does not suffice, for it consists only in substituting one word for another. To declare that memory is a habit is to say that it is an acquired power, an aptitude contracted by the mind; it is to admit, in other terms, that it is one of those faculties whose essence is unknown, which, like the consciousness or like the reason, constitute the mysterious and indefinable nature of the mind.

133. Qualities of a Good Memory. — The qualities of

a good memory constitute a pedagogical rather than a psychological question. We shall content ourselves with the remark that a good memory is prompt in receiving, tenacious in holding, and prompt in recalling its souvenirs.

134. Conditions of the Development of the Memory. — As the facts of memory are not primitive facts, we can lay down the conditions on which their degree and strength depend.

With respect to promptness in receiving, and fidelity in retaining, the conditions are nearly the same.

They consist, in the first place, in the natural intensity or vivacity of the original impression ; and this vivacity itself comes either from the native vigor of the intelligence and the sensibility, or from the novelty or the importance of the object which is presented to the mind. Every one knows by experience that impressions are more or less strong, according as the individual is more or less gifted with respect to his intellectual and sensitive faculties, and also according as the outward appearance, or the moral event which is the object of his consciousness, is more or less considerable and important.

They consist, in the second place, in the degree of attention which we give the individual impressions which are the starting-point of recollections. The more attentive we are, the more quickly and the longer we retain what we wish to learn.

They consist, in the third place, in repetition. Memory, being a habit, has need, like all the habits, of re-enforcing itself by a frequent renewal of the thoughts which it ought to retain.   Usually one single impression does not suffice to fix the recollection.

135. Physiological Conditions. — Memory does not depend alone on psychological conditions. Vigor of health and vitality of organism favor its development. Memory is stronger in the young man than in the old man, not only because the over-accumulation of ideas in the mind of the old man obstructs the acquisition of new recollections, but because his brain is wearied and his vitality enfeebled.   It has often been observed that an old man who recalls with exactness the long-ago events of his youth, forgets the events of the day or of the previous evening.   But it is not merely with age that the memory decreases in power. _At every period of life it can be shown that memory is stronger at certain hours of the day, as on awakening, or after a meal, when the bodily powers have been renewed and refreshed by repose or by food.

136. Laws of the Recall of Recollections. — Vivacity of impressions, attention, and repetition — the physiological conditions which exercise great influence on the first two qualities of memory — have just as evident an effect on the third, that is, promptness in recalling.   It is evident that the recollections that have been acquired with facility, which are durable and tenacious, have contracted, by virtue of this fact, a tendency, in some sort spontaneous, to reappear in consciousness.

But we must push our analysis still farther. Among so many recollections buried in the depths of our memory, which slumber there awaiting the hour of awakening, why do some of them rise to the surface and others not? Why, at a given moment, does one recollection reappear and not another?

It is at this point that there intervenes the association of ideas, the laws of which we shall set forth farther on (see chapter VIII.). The reason why any given state of consciousness, perception, emotion, sensation, or recollection, is succeeded by another recollection, precisely this one and not another, is that there is a bond or relation between the antecedent state of consciousness and the recollection which follows it.

" I am thinking of rain. Why? Because I have seen the sky overcast with clouds. I am thinking of thunder. Why? Because I have seen it lighten. I am thinking of Napoleon I. Why? Because a moment ago I was thinking of Cæsar or Alexander. In all these cases the idea at which I arrived was evidently determined by an antecedent idea. Had the antecedent idea been different, the subsequent idea would also have been different. If, for example, instead of thinking of Alexander, I had thought of Socrates, it is infinitely probable that a moment after I would not have thought of Napoleon." [1]

[1] Rabier, *op. cit.* p. 183.

Recollections, then, are provoked or suggested mechanically, so to speak, by the bonds which connect them with the different states of consciousness which precede them. The association of ideas is the grand law of the recall of recollections.

137. Voluntary Memory. — Nevertheless, the will and the effort of attention also play a part in the recall of recollections. We all know by experience, that with a little reflection we may recover a recollection which escaped us at first, but which we desire to recall. But even in this reflective government of the memory, we need to obey the law of the association of ideas, and we cannot release ourselves from the natural mechanism of the restoration of our recollections. Hence arise those gropings which usually accompany a search for a recollection which has for a long time been blotted from our mind. After a lapse of two years, I am passing by a school called the Seminary of *Polignan*. This name has escaped from my memory and I try to recover it. At first I find nothing; but presently analogous names, *Pompignan*, *Perpignan*, occur to my memory. I reject them, for with the momentary forgetfulness of the true name, there is connected a vague judgment which obliges me to reject the false names, and so, by painful effort and slow degrees, I succeed in reconstructing the exact recollection. And so I have forgotten the name of a person called *Rouquette*, but I have preserved in my mind the idea that his name is almost like that of an animal, a *roquet;* this association of ideas enables me to recover the name I am looking for. So that in the very effort of my will which seeks and finds the recollection it has need of, the association of ideas intervenes as an indispensable element in the success of my pursuit.

138. Ideas which we owe to the Memory. — Memory is not simply the power of recovering our recollections one by one. From the mass of these recollections, through the reflective effort of the mind, there result new ideas which are in some sort real acquisitions of the memory. Such, for example, is the idea of *substance*, which we have already attributed to consciousness, but the conception of which is possible only because the memory gives continuity to consciousness ; the idea of *personal identity;* the idea of *self,* which in reality is but another form of the idea of substance ; and finally, the idea of *duration*, which in turn is but a different translation of the fundamental notion of something which remains the same throughout a succession of changing phenomena.

139. Diseases of the Memory. — The memory, like other human functions, is subject to diseases or disorders which injure and weaken it, or which may altogether destroy it. Sometimes the memory of words is lost, and this disease is called *aphasia;* * it is a physical state which often allows ideas and feelings to continue while forbidding their expression. It may also happen that the memory becomes double ; in the same individual two existences succeed each other, — two states of consciousness, two *Egos.* In one period, the invalid recalls but one series of recollections, and these he forgets in the other period, with which other recollections are connected.

But in its normal state, notwithstanding the multiplicity of individual notions which it contains, and its various species, as the memory of words, of places, of dates, of proper names, etc., the memory is one ; and gives proof of the unity and identity of the mind, without which it would not exist, and which, on the other hand, we would not know without it.

SUMMARY.

67. **MEMORY** is a function of conservation; it preserves and renews in consciousness the knowledge acquired through the other functions of the mind.

68. Memory always supposes a prior consciousness. We recollect only because we have been previously conscious. **RECOLLECTIONS** are secondary or derived facts.

69. The memory which is the continuation or uninterrupted prolongation of consciousness, must be distinguished from the memory which is preceded by forgetfulness.

70. Recollection is often incomplete, and is then called **REMINISCENCE,** while complete recollection is called **RECOGNITION.**

71. The spiritualist philosophers have tried to explain memory by the latent and unconscious existence of recollections ; and the physiologists, by the existence of certain material traces which subsist in the brain.

72. The best explanation, though still insufficient, is that which defines memory as an **INTELLECTUAL HABIT**.

73. The psychological conditions for the development of the memory are :

1. THE VIVACITY OF THE ORIGINAL IMPRESSIONS.
2. ATTENTION.
3. REPETITION.

74. Memory also supposes physiological conditions, as age, health, etc.

75. The recall of recollections depends in great part on the **ASSOCIATION OF IDEAS**. A recollection is suggested through the relation which connects it with the state of consciousness which has preceded it in the mind.

76. It is through the memory that the mind is able to form the ideas of **PERSONAL IDENTITY** and **DURATION**.

CHAPTER VIII

THE LAW OF THE ASSOCIATION OF IDEAS

140. The Association of Ideas. — Properly speaking, the association of ideas is not a special function of the mind ; it is one of its essential laws.   In the succession of its thoughts, and, in general, of all its states of consciousness, the mind obeys the law of association.   In reality, the ordinary expression, "association of ideas," is improper.   It would be better to say, "the association or suggestion of states of consciousness;" for feelings suggest one another as well as ideas.

141. In Reverie. — Let us try to comprehend what takes place in our consciousness when we abandon our thought to itself, when we allow it to follow the course of its reveries freely.   One after another a great number of different representations occupy our mind.   A moment ago we were thinking of the education of our children, and now, without apparent transition, we are thinking of our own duties, or the books we have in preparation ; in an instant, perhaps, we shall be thinking of our fellow-citizens.

Recollections, imaginations, general conceptions, all crowd upon us in apparent disorder in a sort of intellectual swarm.   And yet, if we ascend the series of our thoughts, we shall perceive without difficulty that, like the different links of the same chain, they are all held together by a real, though imperceptible, thread. Our mind passes by invisible bridges from one idea to another. Notwithstanding the superficial confusion of our reveries, there is never any break of continuity in them. Some secret nexus always connects the thought which follows with the thought that precedes.

142. In Reflection. — It is not merely when the thought is unbridled, so to speak, that it obeys the law, in some sense mechanical and fatal, of the association of ideas ; but even when we reflect, when we are the masters of our thought, we are still directed by the law of association.

The recollections which we call up, and the new conceptions which we imagine, respond to our call and present themselves to our mind, only by reason of the bond which unites them to the thought which has served as the starting-point for our reflection. Observe yourselves while you are composing a narrative or a dissertation on a given subject. The ideas and images which you would group in order to make of them the plot of your composition, will all be connected one to another by some thread of relation. Even the most original thoughts which have charmed you by their novelty, as well as the thoughts which are apparently the most fortuitous, have been suggested to you by some relation which associates them with one of your previous thoughts.

143. Classical Examples. — Philosophers have for a long time observed the fact of the association of ideas. Hobbes* relates that one day in a conversation relating to the death of Charles the First, King of England, who had been delivered up to his enemies by treason, an interlocutor suddenly interrupted the conversation by asking the value of a Roman *denarius*. This was a surprise to the listeners, who saw no possible connection between the question asked and the conversation that was in progress. But, nevertheless, the questioner had pursued a logical train of thought. From the treason which had betrayed Charles the First he had passed, by the association of resemblance, to the treason which had betrayed Jesus ; and he wished to know which of these two treasons had been best rewarded.

George Sand * has somewhere written : —

" I have never seen the butterfly Thais flying, without seeing Lake Nemi again ; I have never noticed certain mosses in my herbarium, without again finding myself under the dense shade of the evergreens of Franconia. A little pebble causes me to see again the mountain from which I carried it, and to see it again in its least details from summit to base. The odor of bind-weed calls up before me a wild landscape of Spain of which I know neither the name nor the location, but which I traversed with my mother when I was four years old." [1]

[1] George Sand, *Revue des Deux-Mondes* du 15 Nov. 1863.

Hobbes[1] says again : " From St. Andrew the mind
inneth to St. Peter because their names are read
igether ; from St. Peter to a stone, from the same
iuse, from foundation to church, and from church to
eople, and from people to tumult : and according to
iis example, the mind may run almost from anything
> anything."

Each of us can find similar examples in his own ex-
erience. Sometimes the links which have caused the
liation of our ideas escape us ; but with a little reflec-
on we are almost always able to recover them, and
/en if they remain unknown, we have the right to
firm, in accordance with every analogy, that they still
kist.

144. Intellectual Determinism. — The law of the asso-
iation of ideas obliges us to recognize the fact that in
ie mind everything is coherent, everything has its
onnections. Just as, in the physical world, phenom-
na are derived from and engender other phenomena ;
> in the moral world, thoughts call up one another ;
iey have by their nature, or they contract by accident,
kinship which brings them together. In mind, as in
ature, hazard is an empty term. Each state of con-
ciousness is determined by a previous state of con-
ciousness. There is an intellectual determinism* just
s there is a physical determinism.

145. The Association of Feelings. — Even our feelings,

[1] Hobbes, *Human Nature*, ch. iv.

in their evolution, obey the law of association, not onl
as they suggest all the ideas which are connected witl
the particular emotion that we experience, but also a
they excite, by a sort of affinity, all analogous feelings
Are we angry at something that has happened ?   A
once feelings of malevolence or antipathy arise in ou
hearts against those who are about us, and sometime
against those who deserve it least.   Are we sad ?   No
only will all agreeable and joyous representations b
banished from our imaginations as by fate ; not onl
will sad reflections, by a sort of involuntary selection
be accumulated in our thoughts, but anger, malicious
ness, envy, and discontent with everybody and every
thing, will follow in the train of the initial feeling.   O
the contrary, are we happy ?   Then at once we are over
whelmed with a throng of gentle and joyous conceptions
and our sensibility is invaded by a whole flood of affec
tionate and benevolent emotions.

146. Principles of the Association of Ideas. — Th
association of ideas, or rather the association of ou
states of consciousness, whatever they may be, is the
a fundamental law of human nature.   But how doe
this law act, according to what principles does it exer
cise its power ?   What are the connections, what are
the relations, which usually determine the sequence o
our thoughts and feelings ?

147. Classification of these Principles. — For a long
time philosophers have attempted to reduce to a certair

number of categories, or species, the multiplied relations which may serve as mediums or bonds of union
between our thoughts. The older psychologists distinguished the principles of association into two wide
classes : the first, accidental and superficial ; the second,
logical and essential.

148. Accidental Principles. — Of this number are :

1. *Contiguity in Space.* — We pass from the idea of a
city to the idea of all the adjacent places ; Rome makes
us think of the Forum, of the Campus Martius, and the
Roman Campagna ; Naples, of Vesuvius and Pompeii.
Our thought travels insensibly from one country to
another country adjoining, and from one street to an
adjacent street.

2. *Contiguity in Time.* — Mirabeau makes us think of
the Revolution and of his contemporaries, Louis XVI.,
etc. ; Napoleon III., of the Crimean war, Mexican war,
and the war of 1870. There is here an objective contiguity, so to speak, between the events which have
succeeded one another in time. But there is another,
a subjective contiguity, which brings together and associates two ideas or two feelings, for the simple reason
that they have co-existed or have immediately followed
one another in the mind.

3. *Resemblance.* — This is one of the most fruitful
principles of the association of ideas, and certain philosophers reduce to it all the others. Two contemporary events, or two monuments contiguous in space,

resemble each other because they belong to the same epoch, or because they exist in the same place. But more definite resemblances operate with still greater force. For example, a Gothic church recalls to our recollection all churches of the same description which we have visited, and a school carries back our thoughts to all the schools which we know. It is important to note that the associations founded on the principle of resemblance may be established between the things which are the object of our thought, or between the ideas themselves, or between words. A simple analogy in the sound of words sometimes exposes us to the risk of seeing the current of our thoughts completely turned aside. Many apparent freaks of our imagination, and many of our so-called random thoughts, are due to the consonance of two words very different in meaning, which makes us jump without logical transition from one conception to another.

4. *Contrast.* — Like resemblance, contrast sometimes gives direction to our ideas. We are secretly led, in the presence of a given object, to conceive, not only everything which resembles it, but also all that is in contrast with it. Certain writers, like Lamartine,* always bent on comparisons, obey the law of resemblance ; while others, like Victor Hugo,* who use and abuse antithesis and oppositions, are under the domination of contrast.

149. Rational Principles. — The different principles of

association which we have just enumerated, establish among ideas only relations which are either exterior, or even fanciful, as in the case of the analogy of words. Other principles, on the contrary, bring together two ideas or two facts by virtue of an intrinsic nexus, or of an essential and logical relation.

1. *Relation of Cause to Effect and of Effect to Cause.* — We descend instinctively, so to speak, the ladder which leads from a cause to its effect, and, *vice versa*, we ascend with the same facility from effect to cause. In the presence of a carriage overturned in the street, we think immediately of the events (broken spring, frightened horse, etc.) which have caused the accident. In the presence of a hail-storm which devastates the country, we are naturally led to imagine the effects which will result from it (devastated fields, ruined harvests, broken shrubs, etc.).

2. *Relation of Principle to Consequence.* — A relation analogous to the preceding is that which associates, not simply two connected events, as cause and effect, but two ideas, one of which is a principle and the other its consequence. The relation of principle to consequence is in some sense but a relation of subjective causality. Some one mentions in our presence a philosophical theory, pantheism,* for example; and immediately our mind considers its consequences, as the suppression of human liberty, or the denial of the divine personality, etc. And so we read in some book an apology for regi-

cide ; and we at once catch a glimpse of the principles which gave rise to this consequence, such as contempt for human life, ardent love of liberty, etc.

3. *Relation of Means to End.* — On seeing a machine we ask ourselves what purpose it serves, and, recipro-cally, on considering a manufactured article, we inquire by what means the workman or the machine has pro-duced it. A bird's wing makes us think of flying ; and the harvest, of the grain which was sown. The relation of means to end is hardly more than causality reversed, in the sense that the end is, in reality, the cause of the means employed, and consequently called the final cause.

We might also distinguish the relation of sign to the thing signified. A flag makes us think of the regiment or our country. Smoke evokes the idea of fire, etc.

150. Reduction of these Different Principles. — How-ever exact the preceding enumeration may be, it is per-missible to inquire if all these principles of association may not be reduced or brought back to a smaller num-ber of relations, or even to a single one.

Philosophers long ago attempted this reduction. Aristotle distinguished only resemblance and conti-guity : —

"When we are pursuing a thought that does not pre-sent itself to us immediately, we are led to it by start-ing from another idea by means of resemblance, of contrast, or of contiguity."

Hume admitted three principles : Resemblance, contiguity, and causality. In general, the contemporary English school recognizes but two principles : Contiguity, meaning co-existence or immediate succession of ideas in consciousness, and similarity or resemblance.

But we might go still farther and show that the fundamental, the unique principle of the association of ideas, is subjective contiguity, that is to say, simultaneity or immediate succession in consciousness.

151. The Principle of Contiguity. — John Stuart Mill * clearly expressed this conclusion when he said : "When two impressions have been frequently experienced (or even thought of) either simultaneously or in immediate succession, then whenever either of these impressions or the idea of it recurs, it tends to excite the idea of the other."

In other terms, the one essential principle of the association of ideas is the previous co-existence in consciousness of two feelings or of two conceptions which, having once been brought together, have contracted the habit of always reappearing one after the other.

In support of this theory, it is observed as a fact that all the associations of ideas, on whatever seeming principle they may be founded, have, as a condition, this previous contact, this succession, this simultaneity in consciousness. Contiguity in space is easily reducible to subjective contiguity. As a fact, we pass from the idea of the Capitol to the idea of the Tarpeian Rock, only because, previously, these two ideas were brought into juxtaposition in our mind when we learned Roman history or the topography of Rome. The same is true of the essential relations of causality, of finality, etc. It is evident that we associate with a given effect the idea of a given cause, only because we have already experienced this relation. The principle of causality doubtless suggests to us, in view of every effect, the idea of some possible cause, but it does not teach us what this cause is. If by virtue of the association of ideas we think of this cause rather than another, it is because experience has already presented to us, associated in a succession of thoughts, the effect and its particular cause which we have under our eyes.

152. The Association of Ideas is but a Habit — We are justified, then, in concluding that the association of ideas, understood as the aggregate of the affinities which unite our conceptions, is but a habit — the habit of re-thinking, one after another, the ideas which, once at least, have already been connected in consciousness.

153. The Connection of Ideas. — But beyond this association, wholly mechanical and fatal, as everything is which proceeds from habit, we must recollect that we have the faculty of connecting our ideas logically according to the principles of causality, of finality, etc., which constitute the reason   (See Chapter XII.)

"The association of ideas, properly so called, is a purely mechanical phenomenon which bears no resemblance to that other order of rational and reasonable association which logic and rhetoric require and teach, and which is called the connection of ideas. On the contrary, these two processes are opposed to each other. In order really to connect ideas as the reason requires, we must struggle against the yoke of an extrinsic association of ideas. Poor writers substitute mechanical association for the intrinsic connection of ideas."[1]

154. Association by Resemblance. — There is one single category of associations which we do not seem able to reduce to the law of contiguity. These are the associations, so important and so numerous, and to which poetry is indebted for so many agreeable comparisons — the associations founded on resemblance.

John Stuart Mill himself is willing to admit, in addition to the general law which we have borrowed from him, a complementary law, which may be formulated as follows : " Similar ideas have the power to call up one another." In other terms, apart from all previous association, ideas have a secret tendency to unite, from the simple fact that they have a common resemblance.[2]

155. The Association of Ideas and the Memory. — We

---

[1] Paul Janet. *Traité élémentaire de philosophie*, p. 73.

[2] The partisans of the reduction to unity of all the principles of association do not acknowledge themselves beaten.

" I meet in the street for the first time," says Rabier, " a person who makes me think of a friend who resembles him, who died twenty years ago Here surely is a case where there was no simultaneity of two representations in consciousness, previous to association. Let us analyze this case. The actual representation makes us think of a past representation. Certainly ; but this is because these two representations have marks in common." Rabier, *op. cit.*, p. 191.

now understand how the association of ideas may be considered as the grand law of the recall of recollec tions. United like companions in chains, the states of consciousness form couples, one element of which cannot appear in the mind without a tendency, on the part of the other, to reappear also. The perception of an object reminds us in succession of the different ideas with which it has previously co-existed. One recollection revives another. In other terms, the memory, which is a habit, an acquired disposition to recall an object, is put in play by another habit, the association of ideas, which is an acquired disposition to think of an object in connection with another object.

156. The Imagination — We shall see in the following chapter that the association of ideas does not play a less important part in the development of the imagination. Just as it is the instrument for the restoration of recollections, so we must attribute to it, in great part, the combinations of images which constitute the peculiar products of the imagination.

157. The Reason — Philosophers of the English school go farther; they believe they can explain the necessary principles which govern our thought, by the association or constant concatenation, ever verified in the experience of all men, of the phenomena which succeed one another in consciousness. The relation of cause to effect is but an inseparable association. Farther on (Chapter XII.) we shall state why this theory cannot be admitted.

SUMMARY.

77. THE ASSOCIATION OF IDEAS is an improper expression. It would be better to say the suggestion of ideas, or, still better, the suggestion of states of consciousness.

78. The association of ideas explains in **REVERIE**, and even in **REFLECTIVE THOUGHT**, the transition from one conception to another conception.

79. The succession of our ideas is subject to a true intellectual **DETERMINISM**.

80. Even the feelings are associated, call one another up, and are mutually suggestive.

81. Many principles of association have been distinguished. There are **ACCIDENTAL PRINCIPLES**, like contiguity in space, contiguity in time, resemblance, contrast ; and **LOGICAL PRINCIPLES**, like causality, relation of principle to consequence, and finality.

82. But these different principles may be reduced to one, **SUBJECTIVE CONTIGUITY**, that is, simultaneity, or the previous succession in consciousness of two ideas which henceforth will tend to suggest one another.

83. The association of ideas, then, is but a **MECHANI-CAL HABIT** which the mind contracts by reason of its previous experiences.

84. We must distinguish from the mechanical association of ideas, the logical and rational process which may be called the **INTRINSIC CONNECTION** of **IDEAS**.

85. It does not seem that **ASSOCIATIONS THROUGH RESEMBLANCE** can be reduced to the unique law of contiguity in consciousness.

86. The association of ideas is the law of the **RECALL** of recollections in the **MEMORY**, and of the **COMBINA-TION** of images in the **IMAGINATION**.

CHAPTER IX

THE IMAGINATION AND ITS DIFFERENT FORMS

158. Complex Nature of the Imagination. — In its origin and humble beginnings, the imagination is a function
of conservation like the memory, from which it differs
only in degree. It is then the imaginative memory, the
representative or reproductive imagination; and consists in vividly representing, with the eyes closed, what
has been seen with the eyes open. It is a more vivid
memory, a picturesque memory. We simply recollect
to have seen on a certain day, in the *Jardin d'acclima-
tation*, some of the natives of Ceylon; this is a fact of
memory. But, in addition, we see them again with
their costumes, with their attitudes, with their curious
dances, and with their brown skin which makes them
resemble Florentine bronzes; these are facts of the
imagination.

It is true that the imagination promptly passes this
first stage where it is but the copy of reality. It soon
becomes a function of combination and elaboration; it
modifies in a thousand ways the material which the
imaginative memory places at its disposal; it constructs
and creates; it is finally the inventive or creative imag-

ination, or what might also be called the active imagination.

159. Inventive Imagination. — It is particularly in this
last sense that we generally understand the term imagination. We are ever speaking of its power and fertil-
ity. Now these characteristics belong only to the
second stage of the imagination. *Man of imagination*
is synonymous with poet, inventor, or artist.

160. Importance of the Representative Imagination. —
But we must not disregard the simply representative
imagination, which preserves the exact representation
of the forms and other sensible qualities of objects.
All minds are not equally endowed in this respect.
One man, though having a very acute intelligence and
very expert in abstract reflection, will be incapable of
representing vividly to himself the things which he has
seen, even those which are most familiar to him. Ask
him the color of his friend's hair, or what dress his
sister wore yesterday, and he does not know. He is
lacking in that inner sense of imagination which always
makes us see things as in a picture, — which to the
idea always adds the image. Doubtless this power of
representation is not necessary for the pursuits of the
philosopher, or for the researches of abstract thought ;
but I would not dare affirm that it is not of some service
in the conceptions of the geometrician and in the studies
of the physicist and the chemist. At all events, the
poet, the painter, the sculptor, the musician, and artists

in general, cannot do without it. The painter, even the most original and the most inventive, ought to begin by being capable of seeing objects mentally with their colors and forms. It is useless for certain philosophers to say that the imagination appears only at the moment when it modifies or transforms our recollections; these very recollections may be useful material for the future constructions of the artist and the inventor.

161. The Imagination embraces all the Objects of Sense. — The representative imagination thus collects the material which the creative imagination will afterwards turn to account by virtue of its own peculiar power.

This material is at first borrowed from all the senses, and not merely, as we might at first suppose, from the sense of sight.

Without doubt the greater part of the representations of the imagination are derived from sight, which is the most powerful of all of our senses, the richest in perceptions, and also the one whose recollections are revived with the most clearness. Etymologically, also, the imagination seems to be connected exclusively with the sense of sight. The image is properly the conception of a visual form. It is no less certain that the other senses also give rise to images, that is, to mental representations. The musician imagines sounds and mentally combines them; the compositor imagines the tangible forms of letters, since he recognizes them by

the touch.   Even savors and odors may be represented
by the imagination.

" How many pleasing images have been borrowed
from the fragrance of the fields and the melody of the
groves ; not to mention that sister art, whose magical
influence over the human frame it has been, in all ages,
the highest boast of poetry to celebrate ! " [1]

162. The Imagination and the Inner Emotions. — But
the scope of the imagination would still be too limited,
if we were content to extend it to objects of sense
alone.   We can also imagine afterwards our states of
consciousness, and particularly our emotions, our pleasures, our sorrows, and our passions.   A sorrow long
since forgotten smites my heart and fills my eyes
with tears, when I revisit the place where I first
experienced it.   Poets and novelists evidently have
recourse to the imagination, when they paint with
such vivid colors characters which they invent, and
personages to whom they attribute the different passions of the soul.

Even including abstract and general conceptions,
there is nothing which may not be in some degree an
object of the imagination.   We ascribe life and form
to the most abstract conceptions, as to humanity, to
country, and to nature.   But, in this case, the imagination is no longer representative, but inventive ; it adds
something of its own to the suggestions of memory.

[1] Dugald Stewart, *On the Human Mind.* Part I., ch. viii.

163. Analysis of a Page of Lamartine. — Let us read a page of a poet, and we shall find in it imagination in all its forms : —

"One evening, do you recall it? We were rowing in silence ; there was heard in the distance, on the deep and beneath the sky, only the noise of the rowers, who struck in cadence the harmonious waves."

The imagination of sight and the imagination of hearing are intimately associated in this stanza, which represents to us at the same moment a lake, its waves, the sky, and also the noise of the oars breaking the silence of the night.

"O lake, speechless rocks! grotto! forest obscure! You whom time spares and whom it may restore to youth, beautiful nature, preserve at least the recollection of that night!"

Here the imagination is mingled, so to speak, with abstract thought. At first it personifies nature ; and then it introduces the idea of life, old age, and of possible restoration to youth, — abstract and general ideas in the first degree, — into the representations which the poet makes of the objects of nature.

"Eternity, nothingness, the past, gloomy abysses, what do you do with the days which you ingulf? Speak : restore the sublime raptures which you have ravished from us!"

In these last verses, the poet imagines his past emotions, his love, and the ardent joys of his lost love.

"Let the moaning wind, the sighing reed, the light
perfumes of your balmy air, all that is heard, seen, or
breathed, — let everything say : they have loved."
The imagination of smell appears in the second verse,
associated with images furnished by the other senses.

164. The Proper Office of the Imagination. — The
senses, the sensibility, and the consciousness, and consequently the memory, are thus the sources of the
imagination ; but the imagination proper has its own
activity, which manifests itself by the changes to which
it subjects the elements received from experience.   Let
us try to analyze the different stages of that original
and renovating elaboration from whence proceed the
fictions of the poet, the compositions of the artist, some
of the most important inventions of science, and also
the delicious reveries which charm our life.

165. Additions and Retrenchments. — At first, the imagination proceeds by addition and by retrenchment.
Obedient to its laws, it adds some additional strokes of
beauty to the already beautiful face which recollection
presents to it ; and it clears away from a real landscape
the accidents which mar it and the blemishes which
disfigure it.   Sometimes, doubtless, these additions and
retrenchments, which seem to be original inventions of
the imagination, are but weaknesses or blanks in the
memory, which forgets this or that.   But usually the
modifications introduced by the imagination into the
photographic representation of reality, are deliberate

changes. It is by design that Rabelais * magnifies the
personage of Gargantua, that he gives him eighteen
chins, and that he causes him to be nourished on the
milk of seventeen thousand nine hundred and thirteen
cows. It is by an effort of the imagination, that Swift,*
in his *Gulliver's Travels*, has conceived his Liliputians.

Let us remark, however, that the imagination is more
inclined to enlarge than to lessen. All imaginative
men are inclined to exaggeration and hyperbole.

166. Combination of Different Images. — Most of the
constructions of the imagination are due to associations
or combinations of images borrowed from different
objects. It has been truly said that the imagination
does not create. Its boldest novelties are in reality but
combinations or associations of different elements borrowed from reality. Is it proposed to imagine a character which, in a comedy or in a novel, shall represent
a miser? The poet or the novelist will gather here and
there the different features of avarice which his memory
recalls to him ; he will then place them in juxtaposition,
and will fuse them into one harmonious whole. Is it
proposed to paint or chisel a beautiful face? Here,
again, the imagination of the artist, far from copying
the reality, will combine different images gathered from
experience ; he will combine the eyes of one, the nose
of another, and the brow of a third, etc.

It is to these combinations that must also be referred
the work of the imagination, which consists, as it hap-

pens every moment with the poets, in associating the abstract and the concrete, the intellectual and the sensible. Most metaphors and comparisons are derived from this source. Our imagination is not simply the power of combining into one whole a great variety of images borrowed from sensible reality; but is also the faculty of vivifying our most abstract conceptions by combining with them to material representations.

167. Guiding Principles of the Imagination. — But in this work of combination and construction which particularly characterizes the imagination, the materials are not everything. The poet who creates beautiful characters, and the painter who imagines beautiful figures, must have a guiding idea, *an ideal.* Among all the recollections which a vivid and powerful memory suggests to him, a choice must be made ; and this choice is possible only because the artist pictures to himself a certain ideal.

168. The Ideal. — It is difficult to define the ideal, which is the thing of all others the most difficult to apprehend. We do not take a step in advance by declaring that the ideal is the beautiful. The beautiful itself is a very complex expression which designates a great number of very different things. What likeness is there, for example, between a beautiful poem and a beautiful statue ? (See Chapter XV.) The beautiful is an abstraction by which we designate whatever produces analogous effects on our sensibility, whatever moves us, whatever transports us with admiration.

There are as many kinds of beauty as there are particular and distinct arts. The poet, the musician, the painter, each follows a different idea — the precise idea which is furnished him by his own imagination or by his individual taste, and which varies with the very diversity of natures or temperaments. But if it is difficult to define this idea, this ideal, it is none the less certain that the ideal exists, and that without it, the imagination, the richest in recollections, would be powerless to create, to cast into a mould, or to conform to a type, all the resources which are at its command.

169. Office of the Imagination in the Arts. — Imagination has always been considered the poetic, the artistic faculty *par excellence*. Doubtless the talent of the poet and the artist is eminently a fact of sensibility; but there must be added to vivid emotions a powerful imagination, evoking a great number of recollections and capable of transforming and idealizing them.

Without imagination, art under all its forms would be but the servile photography of reality. But without wishing to speak ill of the literary school which styles itself *realism* * and *naturalism*,* without thinking of depreciating what may be interesting in exact and studious descriptions of nature — descriptions, moreover, which suppose an intense activity of the representative imagination — it is evident that art is something besides a photographic negative of nature. Art idealizes and invents. At one time it creates things that do not exist, and at others it embellishes that which does exist.

" It is nature who furnishes the materials; it is she who gives the marble, the color, the line, the image, the word ; but the imagination of the sculptor, the painter, the poet, adds to them emotion and thought. Out of these combined elements she forms a whole which before did not exist, a body which she animates with her hands when she has found that happy combination which she calls the beautiful."

170. The Imagination in Practical Life. — The imagination also plays an important part in ordinary life. If it sometimes leads us astray and is the source of many errors, it also presents this advantage, that it nurtures our reveries and embellishes reality ; and the delusive and innocent fictions which it suggests to us are like beneficent dreams which sustain us and aid us in supporting the misfortunes of life.

Imagination is the basis of hope and of all those cheerful conceptions with which we love to deck the future. And who would dare deny that hope is one of the essential supports of human activity ? How many poor wretches there are with nothing left but hope, forever sustained by a beneficent imagination. And it is still the imagination which, while vividly representing to us the desired end which must be attained, and while enabling us to multiply means and devices for reaching it, excites our activity, and at the same time renders it fruitful.

And though it may not lead us to any result, it will always have the merit of charming us, of consoling us, of multiplying our joys, and for a moment of suspending our sorrows.

" When in our conception of the future," says Rabier, "the imagination has full course, and, without regard to the real or the possible, spreads before us only the most seductive prospects; she is building, as we say, castles in the air! Let us not speak too harshly of them. There are so many people who have no others!" [1]

171. Imagination and Science. — It is generally supposed that science is the enemy of the imagination. Science, it is said, aspires to the truth, and the imagination is the source of fables and untruths. We forget that the imagination is a supple and flexible faculty which lends itself to a variety of uses. Just as it inspires the poet with his fictions, so it suggests to the scholar the hypotheses which will conduct him to his discoveries.

" Science itself, at least natural science, is impossible without imagination. By means of it Newton * looks into the future and Cuvier * into the past. The grand hypotheses from which grand theories have issued are daughters of the imagination." [2]

1 Rabier, *op. cit.*, p. 201.
2 Paul Janet, *La philosophie du bonheur*, p. 61.

To the same effect Tyndall * has said, —

"There are tories even in science, who regard imagination as a faculty to be feared and avoided rather than employed. They had observed its action in weak vessels and were unduly impressed by its disasters. But they might with equal justice point to exploded boilers as an argument against the use of steam. Bounded and conditioned by co-operant reason, imagination becomes the mightiest instrument of the physical discoverer. Newton's passage from a falling apple to a falling moon was, at the outset, a leap of the imagination." [1]

It is not merely because, in theory, it inspires the scholar with his hypotheses, but it is also because, in practice, it suggests to him his inventions, that the imagination ought to be considered as a useful auxiliary to science. Doubtless, the applications of science are usually the result of studied deduction, or of the logical development of a theory. But in most cases the imagination co-operates in this labor, and by provoking expedients and new combinations, it is the imagination, in part, which prepares the way for practical inventions.

172. Dangers of the Imagination. — But beside the good, there is the bad ; and the detractors of the imagination feel no more embarrassment in pointing out its dangers than its admirers do in setting forth its advantages.

[1] Tyndall, *Scientific Use of the Imagination*, p. 16.

In poetry, and in art in general, it sometimes turns us aside from nature and betrays us into the artificial and the false. In practical life it is the source of the romantic, and by its enchanting fictions it disgusts us with reality. According to the strong expression of Malebranche, the imagination is the *madcap of the house*, the one who throws the home into disorder. Finally, in science, the imagination, Pascal says, is a cheating mistress ; the errors she has inspired are more than the truths she has discovered. She inclines the incautious scholar to dispense with observation and reasoning, and to accept his own reveries for demonstrated truths.

But all the dangers due to the ill-directed use of a disordered imagination to which the reason is not made a counterpoise, ought not to make us forget its benefits and the influence which it exerts upon our faculties. It animates and vivifies the intelligence ; it excites the will ; and at the same time extends the sensibility ; for we really love only the persons and the things whose image is vividly presented to us by the imagination.

SUMMARY.

87. The **IMAGINATION** is a complex function which presents itself under different and very distinct forms. At one time, it is merely a function of conservation, and is then called **IMAGINATIVE MEMORY**, or **REPRESENTATIVE IMAGINATION**. At another, it is a function of combination and elaboration, and it is then the **INVENTIVE** or **CREATIVE IMAGINATION**.

88. The representative imagination accumulates materials for the future combinations of the inventive imagination.

89. The imagination embraces all the objects of sense and also the inner states of the mind.

90. But experience merely furnishes the imagination with the material which it employs ; while the imagination draws from itself the **IDEAL** conceptions according to which it arranges its materials.

91. The proper work of the imagination consists either in **ADDING** or in **RETRENCHING**, or, above all, in **COMBINING** new forms.

92. The imagination plays an important part in the **FINE ARTS.** It permits the artist either to invent outside of nature, or to idealize nature.

93. The imagination is also a **PRACTICAL FACULTY.** It gives inspiration to hope ; it excites activity ; it surrounds us with agreeable fictions.

94. Finally, the imagination has its importance in scientific research, where it suggests **HYPOTHESES** and promotes practical **INVENTIONS**.

95. *Per contra*, the imagination also presents great dangers. It leads the artist astray into the fictitious and the false : it is the source of the **ROMANTIC**; and exposes the mind to all sorts of errors.

X

ABSTRACTION AND GENERALIZATION. ABSTRACT IDEAS AND GENERAL IDEAS.

173. Particular Ideas and General Ideas. — In their proper exercise, the senses and also the consciousness furnish us, at first, only with particular or individual ideas. Doubtless consciousness envelopes and accompanies all the operations of the mind, abstraction and generalization, as well as elementary perceptions. But, in its primitive data, the consciousness, like the senses, suggests to us only particular judgments with reference to a single fact or a single individual.

I am conscious, first of all, say, of a pain which makes me groan, or of a feeling of fear which makes me tremble.

It is only subsequently that, grasping the relation which exists between these different emotions, my mind disengages from them the general idea of sensibility.

In the same way, I perceive through the senses a given tree, then another tree, then a shrub, and finally a plant ; and from these particular perceptions I afterward rise to the general idea of vegetables.

In a word, every perception is particular, that is to

say, relative to a single and definite object. I do not perceive color in general, but the color of such or such an object. I am not conscious of intelligence, but of different intellectual facts.

Particular ideas are, so to speak, the primitive stratum of the intelligence, the first story of our mind. By a subsequent effort which constitutes what is called generalization, we grasp the resemblance of individual objects, or the relations of particular ideas, and we thence conceive general ideas.

174. Concrete Ideas and Abstract Ideas. — But generalization itself supposes a preliminary operation of the same kind, and this is abstraction.

The opposition between the *abstract* and the *concrete* is analogous to that which exists between the *general* and the *particular.* The general idea is always an abstract idea. The particular object which we perceive is always concrete and complex ; it comprises several elements. The color of a rose is perceived along with the form and perfume of that flower. But our mind has the power to consider one of these elements to the exclusion of all the others, either the color, or the form, or the perfume of the rose. Here are three preliminary abstractions, which, compared with other analogous abstractions, with the color, form, and perfume of the lily, the violet, etc., lead us to conceive the general idea of color, form, and odor.

The concrete is whatever the senses make us know

immediately, it is the reality directly perceived. Correctly speaking, the abstract exists only in our thought. The abstract supposes an analysis of the complex elements of reality which the mind considers successively, in such a way as to examine one of them while eliminating all the others.

The concrete, moreover, is not merely the aggregate of material and sensible realities ; the inner facts, the particular phenomena, which consciousness reveals to us one after another, are also concrete facts.

175. Abstraction and Generalization. — It is expedient, then, to distinguish, as distinct operations of the mind, the two intellectual powers called abstraction and gen eralization. Both concur in that elaboration of knowl edge and form a part of those functions of combination, which we have distinguished from the functions of acquisition and conservation.

Abstraction may be defined as *the operation by which the mind, decomposing the complex elements of perception, considers them apart, one after another.*

Generalization is *the operation by which the mind, collecting the analogous or similar elements which a preliminary abstraction has distinguished and separated in a complex reality, arranges and distributes into categories, genera, and species, either the elements themselves (ideas of color, form, savor, odor, etc.), or the individual things in which similar or analogous elements have been successively recognized (idea of humanity, ideas of European, Frenchmen, etc.).*

In other terms, by means of abstraction, we are able successively to detach from the individual objects which we have perceived, the idea of some one of their qualities ; and then, by means of generalization, we combine these successive abstractions in such a way as to form a general idea.[1]

176. Two Forms of the General Idea. — It seems at first sight that there may be two very distinct categories of general ideas. The general idea, in fact, is sometimes the idea of a class of beings or individuals related to one another and resembling one another by some common quality, as *minerals, plants, men,* etc. ; or it may be the idea of these relations, or of that quality common to a great number of individuals, as *reason, sensibility, density, weight,* etc.

177. Extension and Comprehension. — It is to be remarked, however, that every general idea, of either form, contains at once, in different degrees, either the representation of a large number of individuals, or the conception of their common qualities. Thus, the idea of vegetables is, without doubt, primarily the idea of all the objects which can be included under this general appellation ; but it is also, implicitly, the idea of their common qualities (growth, power of nutrition, absence of sensibility, particular structure, roots, stem, flower, etc.).

[1] It is to be observed that the terms abstraction and generalization, like other terms in the vocabulary of psychology, as perception, sensation, etc., represent at the same time both the operation by which the mind abstracts and generalizes, and the results of these operations, that is to say, abstract and general ideas.

So, also, that which dominates in the idea of color, that which is its prominent characteristic, is the reproduction of a quality common to all colored objects. But we cannot think of the color without thinking more or less of the colored objects themselves.

We call the *extension* of the general idea the quality which it has of being applied to a larger or smaller number of individuals (the idea of European, for example, has greater extension than the idea of Frenchman). We call the *comprehension* of the general idea the quality which it has of representing a larger or smaller number of common qualities (the idea of Frenchman has more comprehension than the idea of European).

Extension and comprehension are in an inverse ratio. The more individuals a general idea contains, the fewer common qualities does it represent. *Minerals, animals,* and *vegetables* are general ideas, more comprehensive but less extensive than the idea of *being*, which includes them all, but which is the general idea reduced to its minimum of comprehension.

178. Abstraction and Attention. — Abstraction is one of the conditions of generalization. What, then, is abstraction itself? According to certain philosophers, abstraction is but a form of attention.

"Abstraction," says La Romiguière,* "is not a new faculty to be added to the faculties which constitute the understanding. It is but the attention fixed upon one quality of an object, which, giving this quality a

precedence over the others, separates it in some sense
from them, or abstracts it from them." [1]

It is, nevertheless, true that abstraction is an operation different from attention. And, in fact, in the
greater number of cases, abstraction is instinctive and
irreflective. It is without effort that the mind decom-
poses the elements of reality. It suffices for this purpose that one quality predominate in the objects which
are submitted to the faculties of perception. It is
without attention that the child is struck with the common characteristics of the different specimens of the
vegetable species which present themselves in succession to his notice. Correctly speaking, the attention
plays scarcely any part in the formation of the most of
our abstractions. From analogy, and from some resemblance spontaneously discerned, there springs forth the
abstract idea without reflection.

It is only reflective abstraction which can be confounded with attention. In this case, indeed, the attention which chooses its object, and which, among several
qualities blended in the same perception, considers but
one exclusively — this attention is already an abstraction.

179. Abstraction and Imagination. — If abstraction
has some connection with attention, it is absolutely
opposed to the imagination. To imagine is to determine as fully as possible the representation or the conception of an object ; it is to attribute to it all the

qualities and all the details which characterize it; it is to see it just as it is in reality. By an inverse movement, abstraction simplifies; it suppresses in intellectual representations all the elements which for the moment it does not choose to consider. In other terms, the image approaches reality as exactly as possible; while abstraction, on the contrary, withdraws from it. Hence the divorce which separates poetical minds from scientific minds.

The first are inclined to represent objects integrally, and to omit nothing which makes particular things singular; while the last, on the contrary, are disposed to think only pure ideas, disengaged from the complexity of sense-elements.

180. Different Degrees of Abstraction. — Abstraction may consider either substance apart from its qualities, as the soul, the living being; or qualities apart from substance, as intelligence, sensibility, and will (functions of the soul), or respiration, digestion, and circulation (functions of the living being); or the relation which exists among different qualities, as greatness, smallness, power, weakness, etc.

181. Relations between Abstraction and Generalization. — Though abstraction and generalization, being two distinct operations, are not to be confounded, yet their results, the ideas which are derived from them, are the same. In fact, the abstract idea and the general idea are the same thing.

Some philosophers, it is true, assert that there are particular abstractions.

"It seems therefore," says Reid, "that we cannot generalize without some degree of abstraction, but I apprehend we may abstract without generalizing; for what hinders me from attending to the whiteness of the paper before me, without applying that color to any other object? The whiteness of this individual object is an abstract conception, but not a general one, while applied to one individual only."   ·

It is certain that, by means of the senses, which are the natural instruments of analysis, we are able to perceive in objects their isolated qualities exclusively, as form and color, for example, apart from resistance, odor, and savor; it is certain, also, that through the attention, we may consider the form of a book, apart from its color. But these perceptions, these exclusive reflections, are not, properly speaking, abstractions. In reality, the proper operation of abstraction begins only when the idea of a single quality, distinguished in a complex whole, is associated with the idea of an analogous quality observed in an object of the same class; when, in a word, the idea tends to become general.

There is therefore no occasion for distinguishing abstract ideas from general ideas. Whatever can be said of one is equally applicable to the others.

182. General Ideas and Language. — The question

may be asked, whether, without the use of words, the
human mind can have general ideas. According to a
considerable number of philosophers called *nominalists*,*
words are absolutely necessary for conceiving generalities ; general ideas are but common nouns, —labels
placed on a collection of objects. Properly speaking,
the mind is not capable of thinking the general.

"A general and abstract idea," says Taine, "is a
noun, nothing but a noun, the significant and understood name of a series of similar facts, or of a class of
similar individuals, ordinarily accompanied by the sensible but vague representation of some one of these
facts or individuals." [1]

This is a false and arbitrary opinion. Doubtless
words are necessary for fixing the general idea, for
preserving the recollection of it, and for permitting its
easy handling ; but they are not indispensable in order
that the general idea may dawn upon the mind.

It would be impossible to understand how we attribute a meaning to general words, if we had not in some
degree the power to think the general idea before using
general terms.

This has been forcibly expressed by the Scotch philosopher Hamilton, in the following passage :

" The concept thus formed by an abstraction of the
resembling from the non-resembling qualities of objects,
would again pass back into the confusion and infinitude

---

[1] Taine, *De l'Intelligence*, t. ii. p. 241.

from which it has been called out, were it not rendered permanent for consciousness by being fixed and ratified in a verbal sign. A sign is necessary, to give stability to our intellectual progress, — to establish each step in our advance as a new starting-point for our advance to another beyond.

" A country may be overrun by an armed host, but it is only conquered by the establishment of fortresses. Words are the fortresses of thought. They enable us to realize our dominion over what we have already overrun in thought ; to make every intellectual conquest the basis of operations for others still beyond. Or another illustration : You have all heard of the process of tunnelling through a sand-bank. In this operation it is impossible to succeed, unless every foot, nay, almost every inch, in our progress, be secured by an arch of masonry, before we attempt the excavation of another. Now, language is to the mind precisely what the arch is to the tunnel. Admitting that even the mind is capable of certain elementary concepts without the fixation and signature of language, still these are but sparks which would twinkle only to expire." [1]

It is impossible to characterize more clearly the relations between a general idea and the word which expresses it.

The intelligence doubtless advances without the assistance of words, and grasps the analogies, resem-

[1] Sir William Hamilton's *Lectures*, p. 97.

blances, and relations of things ; but this inner operation would take place to no purpose, it would be fugitive
and perishable, if words did not come to its aid.   Our
mind is so made that it always has need of a sensible
support.   When we perceive natural or particular
objects, it is the thing itself which is represented to
our mind ; but when we conceive the relations of
objects by a purely mental process, our intelligence
needs the support of a word or of a sensible sign.   In
other terms, in the process of abstraction and generalization, words play the same part as the images of particular objects do in the development of perception and
memory.

183. How the Child generalizes. — Whatever may be
said to the contrary, the child is inclined to generalization.   In another place [1] we have quoted examples of this
natural disposition which leads him to generalize according to analogies, sometimes the vaguest and the
most superficial, and also to grasp the real relations of
objects.   Here are some facts which confirm our conclusions on this subject : —

"The son of a learned grammarian, aged five and
one-half years, said to his father : 'There are certainly
feminine verbs !'   'How is that ?' said his father.   ' *To
lay* is a feminine verb, for we always say *she* lays, and
never *he* lays.' " [2]

"A child says *oua, oua*, with reference to a house-

---

[1] See Compayré, *Lectures on Pedagogy*, ch. viii.
[2] Egger, *op. cit.*, p. 51.

dog : and a little time after he says *oua, oua*, with reference to poodles, pug-dogs, and Newfoundlands."

" A child, having learned the words *good boy*, always
put them together ; and when he wished to express the
idea *good cow*, he said *good boy cow*." [1]

The child, then, is unskilful in the use of general
terms, but he does succeed in reaching beyond and
dominating particular and individual perceptions, in
order to grasp their resemblances and relations.

184. Value of General Ideas. — Philosophers have
spent much time in discussing the value of general
ideas ; that is to say, the nature of the realities which
they represent. The *nominalists*, as we have already
remarked, affirm that, being but words or nouns, they
represent nothing. On the contrary, others believe
that to each general idea there corresponds, independently of ourselves, a distinct reality, a substantial entity.
In the Middle Age these were called *realists*. In their
opinion, general ideas, which they call *universals*, are
the only ones which really exist ; while the *nominalists*
maintain that there is no real existence apart from individual things. For the realists, humanity *per se*, or the
ideal type of which men are but the successive copies,
somewhere exists. For the nominalists, there are only
men, with their proper individualities, and a name which
represents them all.

It is difficult to conceive to-day how in the Middle

1 Taine, *op. cit.*, p. 250.

Age there could flourish and be maintained, in opposition to each other, two theses so arbitrary and so equally false in their contrary exaggeration. Realism is no longer anything more than a historical curiosity which no one maintains, and it is a proper source of astonishment that nominalism still has its defenders. The truth is, that a general idea simply represents the relations of objects, or the resemblances common to a larger or smaller number of individuals. This mean and intermediate opinion has been maintained since the Middle Age under the name of *conceptualism.**

185. Simplicity and Clearness of Abstract and General Ideas. — It is wrong to consider the abstract idea as something confused and obscure. On the contrary, the abstract idea, considered in itself, is the simplest and clearest of all ideas. It consists, in reality, in disregarding all accessory circumstances, all that is complex and cumbersome in real perceptions, in order to consider but one single attribute, one single characteristic of natural objects.

"If with the intent to frighten us," said Laromiguière, "one were to propose to us an abstract question, very abstract, we would say, so much the better; it would be all the simpler, all the easier! How have we come to believe in the difficulty of abstract ideas? What is abstract is simple, and what is simple must be easy."

But if abstract and general ideas are, absolutely and in themselves, the simplest of all ideas, they are none the less the most exalted, the highest, and consequently those which the mind has the greatest difficulty in grasping and handling. The summit of mountains is surely the spot where man breathes the best and the easiest ; but before experiencing this sensation of a free and pure air, we must have scaled ascents and climbed rocks. And so, in order to reach abstract and general ideas, we must have passed through a long evolution of intelligence, we must have traversed a great number of intermediate stages. Hence arises the child's repugnance for abstractions, if he has not been prepared to comprehend them ; if his mind has not followed the routes which lead to these final conceptions of human thought.

186. Importance of General Ideas. — It is useless to insist on the importance of general ideas. Every one knows that they are one of the essential conditions of the human mind and of the exercise of thought. Aristotle said, " There is no science of the particular." Science is made only of general ideas. Reduced and limited to its particular perceptions, the human intelligence would scarcely differ from the intelligence of the lower animals. If particular ideas were not collected and grouped into categories by the act of generalization, they would resemble the disbanded soldiers of an army without a chief. Without general ideas, reasoning would be impossible ; for of the two forms of reasoning, one, induction, terminates in general ideas ; while the other, deduction, bases itself on generalizations already accepted by the mind, in order to rise to other generalizations.

187. Dangers of Abstract and General Ideas. — It is nevertheless true that general and abstract ideas may lead the mind astray. By a natural tendency of our intelligence, we are inclined to conceive the existence of a distinct and real object back of each word of our language, and back of each abstraction of our thought. We readily realize our abstractions ; that is to say, we easily believe in the existence of an individual thing corresponding to each of our thoughts. Hence the fables of ancient mythology, which believes in as many Muses as there are different arts ; hence the illusions of the schoolmen, who believed in the existence of humanity *per se*, who multiplied entities and substances, and back of each series of particular objects, back of each abstract quality, saw an occult virtue. But this danger is disappearing more and more with the progress of the scientific spirit and the positive interpretation of nature.

SUMMARY.

96. The functions of acquisition or experience, the **SENSES** and the **CONSCIOUSNESS**, bring us only **PARTICULAR IDEAS** relative to individual objects.

97. It is the functions of elaboration which permit us to disengage from several particular perceptions analogous or

similar elements, and from these elements, by means of association, to form **GENERAL IDEAS**.

98. **GENERALIZATION** is the operation which arranges
in categories or classes, either the qualities common to
several individuals, or several individuals which have common qualities.

99. **ABSTRACTION** is the condition of generalization.
It permits us to decompose complex perceptions in order
to consider apart such or such a quality of objects, by provisionally eliminating from thought all the other qualities.

100. This quality in an object having once been considered
independently, we recognize by comparison an analogous or
similar quality in other objects, and we thus form a general
idea.

101. A **GENERAL IDEA** has more or less **EXTENSION**
and comprehension. Extension is the number of individuals to which it relates; and **COMPREHENSION** the
number of common qualities which it represents.

102. Abstraction is distinct from **ATTENTION**; and is in
absolute opposition to the **IMAGINATION**.

103. Every abstract idea tends to become a general idea;
every general idea is abstract.

104. General terms are necessary, if not to form the general ideas which precede them, which pre-exist, at least to fix
them in the memory and to give them a more precise form.

105. The **NOMINALISTS** are wrong in holding that general ideas are but names; and the **REALISTS** are deceived

when they admit the existence of a distinct entity corresponding to each general idea.   The truth is that general ideas represent the relations of things.

106. Very clear and very simple in themselves, general ideas are difficult for every mind that has not traversed the intermediate stages which lead to them.

107. There is no science without general ideas; **GENERALIZATION** is the condition of scientific procedure.

108. General ideas may lead us astray, if we realize them apart from our mind.

CHAPTER XI

JUDGMENT AND REASONING

188. Different Senses of the Word Judgment. — In ordinary language, judgment is almost always synonymous with accuracy of mind. To say of some one that he is a man of judgment, is to affirm that he has good sense, that he easily distinguishes the true from the false.

" Judgment," says Kant, "is the distinctive characteristic of what is called good sense, and the lack of good sense is a defect which no study can repair. We may indeed offer to a man's understanding a supply of rules, and graft upon it, in some degree, that foreign knowledge ; but the pupil must already possess for himself the faculty of using it correctly. A doctor, a judge, a publicist, may have in their heads many pathological, judicial, and political rules, and yet fail in the application of them, because they have not been trained to that sort of judgments by examples and real affairs."

In this sense, judgment supposes not only a natural rectitude of mind, but also the exercise of reason. It is an aggregate of intellectual qualities, the most precious of all perhaps, since they constitute upright and accurate minds, — qualities which the education of the intelligence ought particularly to propose for an end.

But the signification of the word judgment, in psychology, is very different. To the psychologist, judgment is synonymous with affirmation ; it is the act by which the mind affirms this or that. The grossest error is a judgment, and minds most addicted to falsehood judge as much, if not as well, as sound minds.

189. Judgment and Proposition. — Judgment may therefore be defined : *an intellectual operation by which the mind affirms, either the existence of an object, or the relations of two ideas.* The verbal expression of a judgment is the proposition, and so deductive reasoning is an intellectual operation, and its verbal expression is the syllogism, that is to say, a series of three propositions.

In every proposition there are three terms, the subject, the verb, and the predicate. The subject is the person or thing spoken of ; the predicate is the quality which limits the subject ; the verb is a copulative word which unites the subject and the predicate.

And so in every judgment there are three elements : the idea of the object (person or thing) which we qualify ; the idea of the quality which we attribute to that object ; and the act of affirmation by which the mind declares that the quality belongs or does not belong to the object.

190. Judgment the Essential Act of the Mind. — We

have already shown (Chapter IV.) that judgment is the essential operation of the intelligence. As Rousseau has said, "The distinctive faculty of an intelligent being is the power to give a meaning to the little word *is*."

In fact, the verb *to be* is the verb *par excellence;* in a sense, the unique verb. The other verbs, the predicate verbs, are but the fusion into a single word, (1) of an idea, as the idea of some act or state, and (2) of the verb *to be*, expressing the affirmation.

191. Different Kinds of Judgments. — Judgment, then, is not a special function of the intelligence. In reality, every act of the intelligence terminates in a judgment. To perceive, to imagine, to conceive, to recall, to reason, all this is to think, and at the same time to judge.

Consequently, there are different species of judgments. We might enumerate as many kinds of judgments as there are functions of the intelligence; and in this sense we might distinguish the judgments of conscience, the judgments of the senses, those of the memory, of the imagination, and of the reason.

But, from whatever intellectual source they proceed, judgments present, in the form of the propositions which express them, differences which permit us to distribute them into a certain number of categories.

192. Affirmative Judgments and Negative Judgments. — With respect to *quality*, judgments are ordinarily distinguished as *affirmative* or *negative*, according as the propositions which interpret them show the agreement or disagreement of two ideas. But negative judgments are such only in form ; in reality, they always include an affirmation, — the affirmation that the subject and the predicate do not agree with each other.

193. General Judgments and Particular Judgments. — With respect to *quantity*, judgments may be *particular* or *general*. General judgments are judgments which have for subject a word which designates an entire class of beings or objects : "All men are mortal" — "all bodies are extended." The subjects of particular judgments, on the contrary, are applicable to only a portion of the class of the beings or things under consideration : "Some men are liars" — "some bodies are luminous." From this point of view, we might also distinguish *individual* judgments, which are applicable only to a single individual.

The distinctions just indicated are *formal* distinctions, derived from the form of the propositions.

Other distinctions of more importance proceed from the intrinsic characteristics of judgments.

194. Primitive Judgments and Derivative Judgments. — Judgments may be distributed into two classes, according as they result immediately from the functions of acquisition or intuitive perception ; or as they proceed from a reflective comparison of two ideas previously acquired. The first are *primitive*, and the last *derivative* judgments.

"As I am speaking, the sun shines," "the snow is falling," "it thunders." These are primitive or immediate judgments.

"The sun is immovable," "snow is frozen water," "thunder is an electrical phenomenon." These are derivative judgments.

The old psychology restricted the term judgments to derivative judgments. Every judgment, it affirmed, supposes a reflective comparison between two ideas previously acquired. It is now generally admitted that, from their earliest manifestation, the senses and the consciousness give rise to real judgments which consist at least in affirming the existence of an object or of a phenomenon.

195. Judgment and Belief. — In its affirmations, the judgment is determined from *evidence*, that is to say, from a clear and exact perception of an object or of the relation of one object to another.

The judgment, moreover, is sometimes true and sometimes false. Error, like truth, is a judgment. Judgment is therefore the same thing as *belief.* Believing, judging, and thinking, are synonymous terms.

196. Definition of Reasoning. — Reasoning, like judgment, is a distinct operation of the mind, an intellectual act irreducible to any other. In the activity of the intelligence there are three stages, three essential moments : conceiving or having ideas ; judging or associating conceptions ; reasoning or connecting judgments.

Just as judgment is the assemblage of two ideas united by an act of affirmation expressed by the verb *to be*, — so reasoning is a series or combination of judgments brought together in such a way that the latter seems like the legitimate conclusion and necessary consequence of the former.

197. Conditions of Reasoning. — Reasoning, therefore, involves three previous and distinct operations. It supposes (1) a clear conception of the ideas which are to be the material of the process; (2) in the previous judgments an affirmation of already known relations between these ideas; (3) an attentive comparison of these affirmations themselves, one with another.

The proper act of reasoning will consist in deriving from this comparison a new judgment implicitly contained in the preceding judgments; and for this purpose the reasoning is based on principles derived from the reason. (See Chapter XII.)

198. Verbal Expression of Reasoning. — We have already remarked that just as the judgment finds its verbal expression in a proposition, so reasoning, rigorously expressed, gives rise to the *syllogism*, that is to say, to an argument constructed of three propositions. *God is perfect; goodness is a perfection; God is therefore good.* In every syllogism, as in the one taken for an example, there are three ideas : *God, goodness, perfection.* One of these ideas serves as an intermediate term, or term of comparison between the other two; in the above example it is the idea of perfection.   This is called the *middle term*.   With this idea of perfection we compare one after another the two other ioeas, which we call the *major* and the *minor* term, *God* and goodness ; and after having assured ourselves from an examination of these two primary judgments, called premises, that there is agreement or accord between the idea of perfection and each of the other two, we affirm, in the conclusion, that there is also agreement or accord between the idea of God and the idea of goodness.

In a word, we apply to the comparison of ideas the mathematical axiom which says, " If each of two quantities is equal to a third, they are equal to each other." Without entering into further details, and without attempting to expound the complicated theory of the syllogism, let us add that each of the two premises has a special name ; the one containing the *major* term is called the *major premise*, and the one containing the *minor* term, the *minor premise*.

199. Reasoning and the Syllogism. — The syllogism, therefore, is not the same thing as reasoning. We must be careful not to confound the inner act of the mind which judges and reasons, with the verbal translation which it gives to it in language.

All reasonings, however, do not allow themselves to be expressed in a form as simple and concise as the syllogistic argument.   In most cases of reasoning the premises are far more complicated than in elementary syllogisms like the one we have quoted. Usually there are several minors, and consequently the comparison of the premises is delicate and difficult. The mind comes to the conclusion only at the expense of a great effort of attention.

On the other hand, it is rare that the thinker who reasons, even the most rigorously, imposes on his reasoning the syllogistic form. In conversation, in discourse, and in books, we rarely use the syllogism, which, on the score of clearness and precision, cannot atone for what is heavy and pedantic in it. But even in scientific treatises, writers have long since renounced the syllogistic forms which the theologians of the Middle Age had attempted to bring into vogue. There is no occasion, therefore, to give excessive attention to the intricate rules of the syllogism. The minute and profound study made of it by the logicians may interest those who would make an exhaustive study of the play and mechanism of reasoning; but it is more curious than useful, and, practically, it can hardly presume to develop the art of reasoning.

200. Induction and Deduction. — What is more important is to inquire, whether, in reality, there are one or more distinct forms of reasoning.

All psychologists and logicians distinguish *induction* from *deduction.*

Induction rises from particular truths to general

truths, from fact to law ; deduction, on the contrary, descends from general truths to particular truths, from principle to consequence. Or, rather, induction proceeds from a part to the whole, from the less to the greater. Deduction follows an inverse order. To deduce is to exchange a piece of gold for the smaller pieces which represent its value ; induction is an operation of greater difficulty, and at first sight inadmissible and impracticable ; for it consists in realizing with a few silver pieces of lesser value a gold coin of great value.

201. Induction and Deduction in the Sciences. — Let us explain still further the difference between inductive reasoning and deductive reasoning. We shall thence discover whether the difference is as real as it appears.

In the sciences of observation and experiment, induction is the universal rule. When the facts have all been observed and established, we generalize. We affirm that heat will always and everywhere expand the bodies subjected to its influence ; that a stone free to move under the action of gravitation will fall at all times and in all places. From a simple observation, sometimes from a single one, but more often repeated several times, we pass to a universal affirmation.

In the abstract and exact sciences, deduction is almost exclusively employed. Starting from acknowledged axioms and definitions, we search for their consequences. From the definition of a triangle or a circle, by the aid of certain axioms, we derive a series of theorems. Here the process of reasoning is manifestly legitimate, for it consists simply in bringing to light the truths contained in principles already admitted.

202. Induction brought back to Deduction. — Though the two forms of reasoning seem to provoke the mind to two opposite movements, the logical process is essentially the same in both cases.

In reality, in every deduction there is an unexpressed general truth, the common major term of all inductive reasoning. This is the rational belief in the order, constancy, and uniformity in the succession of phenomena. When the physicist, after having seen two or three kinds of matter expand under the influence of heat, confidently declares that all bodies placed under the same influence will undergo the same modifications, it seems at first sight that the sole ground of his induction is the short series of facts which he has observed. But this is far from being true. That which really authorizes the scientist to accept the general, the universal law which he has established, is the principle previously stated, namely, the uniformity of nature.

In other terms, all inductive reasoning may be brought back to a syllogism in the following form: The same causes produce the same effects (major); I have proved in three cases that the phenomenon A was the cause of phenomenon B (minor); hence, always and everywhere, A will have B for its effect.

203. Differences which Persist. — Induction and deduction, then, are but two manifestations, two different forms of the same logical operation. This, however, is not a reason for forgetting that each process has its own special rules and laws which are studied in the two fundamental divisions of all logic, inductive logic and deductive logic.

204. Rules for Induction. — For induction, it is first necessary to be assured, by exact observations and skilful and repeated experiments, that we do not confound the accidental coincidence of two phenomena with their constant relation.

205. Rules for Deduction. — For deduction, we must be careful to admit only clear and exact definitions, and principles which are either self-evident truths, that is to say, axioms, or inductive laws scrupulously verified.

206. Importance of Reasoning. — When we know the nature and different forms of reasoning, it is easy to comprehend the importance of this intellectual operation. Without reasoning, human knowledge would be confined within the narrow circle of the immediate intuitions of the reason and of the direct perceptions of experience. Human intelligence would be forbidden to pass beyond the limited horizon of the senses, and to conceive the general laws which constitute science, and by which the mind embraces the entire universe.

On the other hand, it must not be forgotten that we may make an abuse of reasoning ; that too much logic leads us astray and deceives us ; and, finally, that it is sometimes true to say of the human mind what Molière said of the house of the *Learned Ladies:* "that reasoning banishes reason from it."

Excess in the use of deductive logic especially, and excessive application of reasoning to any and every subject, may, from consequence to consequence, lead us on to conclusions which, though regularly deduced, are nevertheless contrary to our interests and needs, and in opposition with facts.

SUMMARY.

109. JUDGMENT, in the psychological sense, is the intellectual operation which consists in **AFFIRMING** the existence of an object, or the relation of two ideas.

110. The verbal expression of a judgment is the **PROPOSITION**. It consequently consists of three elements, represented by the **SUBJECT**, the **PREDICATE**, and the **VERB** which joins the predicate to the subject.

111. The act of judgment is expressed by the verb **TO BE**.

112. Judgment is the essential operation of the mind.

113. According to the propositions which express them, **JUDGMENTS** may be distributed into several categories, as **AFFIRMATIVE** or **NEGATIVE, GENERAL, PARTICULAR,** or **INDIVIDUAL.**

114. Considered in their origin, judgments are either **PRIMITIVE,** — those which result immediately from the faculty of perception, — or **DERIVATIVE,** — those which come from a previous comparison of two ideas.

115. REASONING is also an intellectual operation irreducible to any other, and consists in grasping the relation of two or more judgments.

116. The verbal expression of reasoning is the **SYLLO-GISM**. It comprises three propositions: the first two are called **PREMISES**, and the last is called the **CONCLU-SION**, or the consequence of the other two.   .

117. Reasoning presents itself under two forms, **INDUC-TION** and **DEDUCTION**.

118. INDUCTION consists in passing from fact to law, from particular truths to general truths. **DEDUCTION** follows the inverse movement, and descends from principle to consequence, from general truths to particular truths.

119. Induction may nevertheless be brought back to deduction ; for all inductive reasoning supposes, as an unexpressed major premise, this rational truth: "The same causes produce the same effects."

120. REASONING is one of the essential conditions of the development of the intelligence, which without it would remain confined within the narrow circle of immediate experience.

CHAPTER XII

THE REASON; NOTIONS AND FIRST TRUTHS

207. The Reason and the Other Functions of the Intelligence. — When we have enumerated the different functions of acquisition from which the mind is nurtured, and the different functions of elaboration which are the derived channels through which the reflective effort of the mind conducts the thought, there still remains something else to be explained in the intelligence; there remains a residuum which can be accounted for neither by the faculties of experience nor by the faculties of combination, — a substratum of ideas and truths which an analysis of the ideas and judgments furnished by the other faculties does not succeed in reaching, and which is precisely what philosophers call the *reason.*

208. Different Senses of the Word Reason. — At the first glance, we are surprised at the diversity of meanings which language seems to give to the word reason. .Thus, in certain cases, reason simply signifies the sound state of the mind as distinguished from unreason or madness, as when we say of a madman, *he has lost his reason.* In other cases, we mean by reason, accuracy

of judgment or sobriety of views : *this orator speaks reasonably ; this doctrine is full of reason.*   Again, reason
is the opposite of instinct ; it is the reflective activity
of man, as distinguished from the instinctive activity
of the animal : *animals are deprived of reason.*

Finally, and it is in this sense that we here employ
the term, reason is the word which designates the highest of the intellectual faculties, that which reveals to
us universal, necessary, and absolute ideas.   In this
sense, it is opposed to experience, that is, to the senses
and the consciousness.   *The idea of color is derived from
the sense of sight ; the idea of self comes from consciousness ; the idea of the good, and the idea of the infinite,
have their source in the reason.*

209. Reduction of the Different Senses. — If, however,
we reflect on the subject carefully, we shall be convinced that this diversity of significations is more
apparent than real, and at bottom we everywhere find
the same reason, differently modified.

In fact, the reason is an aggregate of notions and
affirmations, of ideas and judgments, of conceptions and
principles, which preside over the intellectual development of man.   It is because it obeys these principles
that the mind moves forward correctly, normally, and
that it escapes madness and folly.   It is also because it
supports itself on these principles, that the mind is
capable of directing its ideas and of governing its intellectual conduct.

It is then always the same reason which, in man, is opposed to the aberrations of mental alienation, or to false judgments, or to the irreflective impulses of instinct.

210. Reason in the Child. — It would be wrong to regard the reason as a faculty peculiar to mature age, whose appearance is tardy in the evolution of the mind. The infant already possesses and often manifests the tendencies of that reason which is common to all men, which lightens every intelligence coming into the world. When a child demands the how and why of things, he obeys the instinct of a reasonable being who wishes to know the causes of all he sees. Doubtless he will be incapable of formulating the principle of causation, and will even understand but little about it, if you explain it to him. But without knowing it, by an impulse still unconscious and instinctive, he is ever applying the principle of causality.

And so the primary notion of space imposes itself on his conceptions.

"One of my sons," says Egger, "seven years of age, was one day looking with me for an object which he had lost. As we did not succeed in finding it, he said to me : 'Something must always be somewhere.' Under a very artless, but still a very clear form, this is the idea that all matter occupies a place in space. I had certainly never attempted to teach him this. The general formula was disengaged all by itself and without any special effort, as far as I could see, from the observation of a particular fact." [1]

Here is another example, borrowed from the same author : —

"Felix, aged seven years and nine months, asks his mother: 'Before the world what was there?' 'God who created it.' 'And before God?' 'Nothing.' To which the child replies: 'There must have been a place where God is.' " [1]

211. The Conscious Reason. — At first latent and confused, the reason in the adult and in the man becomes conscious of itself. Through reflection it analyzes itself and succeeds in formulating clearly the laws which govern the mind. "We must distinguish," says Leibnitz, "between the abstract and formal expression of the principles of reason, and the real possession of these principles under a confused and obscure form."

The laws of the reason have received different names from philosophers. They have been called, in turn, common and universal notions, innate ideas, first truths, necessary truths, truths à *priori*, categories of the intelligence, constituent and regulative principles of the intelligence, etc. We prefer to adopt the expression, notions and first truths.

212. Notions and First Truths. — The notions and truths which are derived from the reason are called

---

[1] Egger, *Observations sur le développement de l'intelligence chez les enfants,* p. 65.

'rst, because they are the very conditions of all intel-
:ctual activity, and the principles which make possible
ll the operations of thought. "Logically," says Leib-
itz, "particular truths depend on more general truths
f which they are but the examples." Doubtless they
o not appear first chronologically; for it is experi-
nce which provokes them to appear and to disengage
1emselves. But nevertheless they exist previous to
xperience. They are the natural data of the mind,
1gically prior to the data of the senses and of
2nsciousness.

213. Distinction between Notions and First Truths.—
Iotions are simply ideas : truths are judgments. But
1e distinction is more apparent than real; for first
leas are almost necessarily accompanied by belief.
Ve cannot think of *causality*, that is, of the necessary
ependence of events, without affirming that it exists ;
or of *substance*, that is, of the permanent basis of
1ings, without believing that there is substance.

214. Characteristics of First Truths.

1. First truths are *universal*. This universality is to
e understood in two senses. First truths exist in all
1telligences, and at the same time they are applicable
2 all existences. They are common to all minds, and
: is of them that Descartes intended to speak when he
aid that good sense is the thing of all others the most
7idely distributed. They are in the mind, said Leib-
itz, what the muscles and tendons are in the body.

On the other hand, universal truths, at the same tim
that they govern all intelligences, have their applic
tion everywhere and always.   It is not merely of actua
facts, the facts which are taking place to-day or tha
will take place to-morrow, that we assert that they hav
a cause; but of every event whatever it may be, —
whenever and however it may take place.

2. In the second place, first truths are *necessar*
We not only affirm that every phenomenon has a cause
but it is impossible for us to conceive the contrary.   I
is not necessary that the death of a man have any de
terminate cause, as illness, murder, or suicide, but i
is necessary that it have a cause.

"We not only judge in this way in all cases, natur
ally and by the instinctive force of our understanding
but try to judge otherwise, and, in the case of a give
phenomenon, try not to suppose a cause for it.   Yo
cannot do it.   The principle of causality is not onl
universal, but it is necessary."[1]

3. In the third place, first truths are *self-evident*
We cannot demonstrate first truths; they cannot b
connected with previous principles, since they ar
themselves first principles, the conditions and bases o
all demonstrations.

"None of these things," says Pascal, "can be demon
strated; but the cause which makes them incapabl
of demonstration is not their obscurity, but, on th

[1] Victor Cousin, *Cours de l'histoire de la philosophie*, t. iii., p. 154.

contrary, their extreme evidence ; this lack of proof is not a defect but rather a perfection."

And Pascal concludes that, " in axioms we must look only for things which are perfectly self-evident." But we must avoid counting among axioms or first truths, truths which are doubtless rational, but which can be demonstrated. Thus, Leibnitz has observed that it is wrong to consider as an axiom the truth that *two and two make four*, since it can be demonstrated by defining the numbers two, three, and four.

215. Enumeration of First Truths. — Without pretending to give in this place a complete enumeration and a definitive classification of the essential elements of the reason, we ought to indicate the principal ones, and at the same time denote their place and functions in intel lectual activity.

But it is necessary to make a preliminary distinction, that between the practical reason and the pure reason.

216. The Practical Reason. — In fact we must sharply distinguish between the rational principles relative to practice and to moral conduct, which Kant calls the *practical reason*, from the rational principles relative to pure science and to theoretic speculation, which he calls the *pure reason*.

The practical reason is nothing more than the aggregate of notions and affirmations commonly designated by the term, *moral consciousness*. That there is a natural and absolute difference between right and wrong ; that there is a necessary obligation to do what is right, or, in other terms, that there is such a thing as duty ; and, finally, that he who does right deserves esteem, and that he who does wrong forfeits esteem, — these are about the contents of the practical reason ; these are the foundations of ethics.[1]

217. The Pure Reason. — The pure reason is that which regulates the exercise of our speculative faculties, which governs and determines our scientific researches. It is the pure reason also which leads us on, as to a court of last appeal, to the idea of an ideal, perfect, and absolute being, God.

Here again it is necessary to make a distinction : namely, between first truths which regulate thought in its relations with objects, and first truths which concern thought only in its relations with itself.

1. On the one hand, thought in itself obeys certain laws of its own, certain logical axioms without which it could not come to an understanding with itself. These principles are : (1) The principle of *identity*, which is equivalent to saying, " What is is." This is the principle which the Greek sophists called in question when they claimed the right, on the same subject, to pass from affirmation to negation, and conversely.

" ' How you go on, always talking in the same way, Socrates ! ' ' Yes, Callicles, and not only talking in the same way, but on the same subjects. . . . But I re-

---

[1] On this subject see Compayré. *Eléments de Morale.*

proach you with never saying the same about the same things, for at one time you were defining the better and the superior as the stronger, then again as the wiser, and now you bring forward a new notion.' Plato thus opposes the unity of true science, in which whatever is, is so always while the same reasons exist, to that multiple and changeable science of the sophists, which remains fixed neither in the substantial nor the intelligible." [1]

(2) The principle of *contradiction*, which is derived from the principle of identity, and is stated as follows : *A thing is not different from itself.* [2]

"The principle of contradiction," says Cousin, "is the rock of all certitude. To destroy it is to destroy every principle, every judgment, every reasoning, every proposition, every perception of consciousness, every thought."

2. On the other hand, without the reason, science would be but a barren accumulation of facts without connection and without laws, — of isolated experiences without cohesion. It is the reason alone which permits the scientist to establish necessary relations among phenomena. It makes provision for this task by three principles: the principle of causality, the principle of substance, and the principle of induction. These are

---

[1] A. Fouillée, *Philosophie de Platon*, t. ii., p. 37.

[2] It is usually expressed thus: "A thing cannot be and not be at the same time ; or, a thing must be or not be ; or, the same attribute cannot at the same time be affirmed and denied of the same subject." — *Vocab. of Phil.*

in some sense objective principles, since they are applicable to objects.

218. Principle of Causality. — The principle of causality may be formulated as follows : *Whatever begins to exist has a cause.*

In other terms, the human mind admits of no solu-tion of continuity in the successive order of phenomena. Whatever begins to exist must have its explanation, its principle, its *raison d'être*. In its last analysis, scientific research has no other end than to determine the causes of facts. It is observation and experience which discover to us, in each given case, the particular cause which is at work ; but it is the reason which affirms in advance that there is a cause, whatever may be its nature.

219. Principle of Substance. — The principle of substance is stated as follows : *Every quality supposes a substance.* Or, again : *Everything which changes supposes something which endures, which does not change.*

220. Principle of Induction — The reason also imposes on us a law to believe in an immutable order in the uni-verse, in a necessary constancy in the relations observed among phenomena.

This is what is called the principle of induction, and is formulated as follows : *Uniformity of succession is the law of nature ;* or : *There is order in the universe ;* or, again : *The same causes produce the same effects.*

221. Other Principles — We might add other princi-ples to the list which we have just drawn up : for example, the principle of final causes, which is thus stated : Whatever happens has a purpose ; or : Nothing is pro- duced without a purpose. But this principle is neither universal nor necessary. In a great number of cases we do not believe that things have a purpose, an end. The uneven configuration of a mountain doubtless has an efficient cause ; but has it a purpose, a final cause ? Moreover, the principle of final causes is connected with a prior belief, with the belief in God, with the idea of providential design, or of an intelligent organ- izer of the world. It is not then a first truth, but merely a derivative truth.

We may also connect with the reason the notions of space and time : *Every body is in space ; Every event takes place in time.*

222. The Infinite. — Finally, the office of the reason is not merely to regulate the acts of the moral life and to co-ordinate the experiments of scientific research. It is also the source of notions which constitute meta- physical science, the sum total of which permits us to conceive of the existence and nature of God. It aspires to something else than the direction of the intelli- gence in the real world. It introduces us into the ideal world, and makes us conceive, over and above the things which are contingent, relative, imperfect, tran- sient and finite, the necessary, absolute, perfect, eternal and infinite being who is the cause of causes, the prin- ciple of order in the universe, and the principle of good in the consciousness.

223. Nature and Origin of the Reason. — The reason having once been defined, it remains to inquire if it is, as most philosophers believe, an absolutely original element of the intellectual constitution of man ; or, on the contrary, as some modern thinkers assert, either an extract or an abstract of experience, or the result of heredity, — the slowly acquired product of the toil of the intelligence through the centuries.

224. Empiricism. — We call *empiricism* or *sensualism* the philosophical doctrine which explains first ideas by experience. According to the sensualists, the mind is at first but a *tabula rasa*, — a tablet whereon nothing is yet written ; the intelligence is absolutely void of the disposition or inclination to think in one way or in another.

Experience, by way of abstraction, induction, and generalization, produces all our ideas ; and the characteristic of necessity and universality presented by first truths comes entirely from the constant repetition of the same experience. From having seen causes produce effects, we come to affirm that every phenomenon has a cause.

225. Idealism. — As opposed to empiricism, *idealism*, under different forms, believes in reason as a distinct faculty ; but the explanation which it gives is bad. Plato resorted to *reminiscence*. The soul had lived a prior life where it had seen first principles face to face ; the notions of the reason, consequently, are but recollections.

Malebranche believes that through direct intuition we see rational truths in God.

Finally, some other philosophers seem to believe that the principles of the reason are innate; "like so many marks which God has imprinted on our soul," from which it would seem to follow that notions and first truths present themselves spontaneously to our mind without effort, without a preliminary evolution of the intelligence, and without any aid from experience.

226. Modern Empiricism. — Modern philosophers, and especially those of the English school of which John Stuart Mill is chief, have revived sensualism by trying to explain first truths by the association of empirical ideas. According to them, the necessity of the idea of cause, for example, is merely the result of constant association, ever verified by experience, of the succession of causes and effects Besides, these philosophers invoke the action of heredity. The inseparable associations from which are derived the so-called first truths, are confirmed from century to century by the experience of successive generations, and are gradually transformed into hereditary habits.

There is but one thing to say to this doctrine; and this is, that experiences, however numerous and however often they may be repeated, cannot be substituted for the universality and absolute necessity which are the characteristics of first truths.

"Experience," says Paul Janet, "is very far from

giving us an inseparable association of cause and effect.
. . . How many phenomena there are whose antecedents
we do not know! The number of cases in which we
can demonstrate the causal relation is very small compared with the number of cases in which a demonstration is impossible." [1]

As to the effects of heredity, it is equally impossible
to comprehend how an accumulation of experiences,
even continued through several centuries, could transform contingent truths into necessary truths. The
contingent, though added to the contingent forever,
will never give the necessary.

227. The True Solution. — The true solution is that of
Leibnitz and of all the philosophers who admit the con-
currence of experience with the native constitution of
the intelligence. Experience does not bring us the
notions and rational truths which infinitely surpass it,
since it can make us comprehend only the things which
are limited and contingent; while the affirmations of
the reason are universal and necessary. But if experience is not the source of rational ideas, it is the occasion of their development; it is experience which in
some sense reveals them, and which causes them to
issue from their latent condition.

" Rational beliefs," as Rabier justly remarks, "are
born of the commerce of the spirit with things; they
are due neither to brute experience nor to pure spirit,

---

1 Paul Janet, *op. cit.*, p. 217.

but at once to experience and intelligence, — to an intelligent *empiricism*."

In other terms, the mind, as Leibnitz has said, contains within itself the principle of many notions and
truths which are revealed by external objects. Doubtless we cannot read in the soul the eternal laws of the
reason at sight, as the edict of the Prætor * is read from
the scroll, without the trouble of an examination ; but
it is enough that we can discover them within us by the
use of attention, with the data furnished by the senses.

The ideas and truths of the reason are innate, like
the inclinations. dispositions, habits, and all our natural
potentialities ; like the concealed veins which leave a
trace in a block of marble.

It is in the same sense that Diderot said, in reply to
the sensualist Helvetius : "The soul of man is not in
his senses, as that of the eagle is in his eye, or that of
the dog at the end of his nose. Sensations are like the
spark which sets on fire a barrel of alcohol but is extinguished in a bucket of water. For thousands of
centuries the dew of heaven has fallen upon rocks without making them fertile. The pick of the miner who
digs in the mines of Golconda * does not produce the
diamond which it unearths."

SUMMARY.

121. The faculties of acquisition, and the faculties of combination or elaboration, do not suffice to explain the whole of mind.

122. The **REASON**, in its psychological sense, is the aggregate of notions and truths which are derived neither from experience nor from the combinations of experience.

123. The reason, at first latent, confused, and obscure in the child, comes only little by little to formulate its principles in a precise and conscious way.

124. The reason comprises both **NOTIONS** and **TRUTHS**, that is, ideas and judgments.

125. These are called **FIRST TRUTHS** or *à priori* truths, because they are the fundamental principles of the intelligence.

126. First truths are **UNIVERSAL** and **NECESSARY**; universal, because they exist in all minds, are applicable to all objects; and necessary, for the contrary of what they affirm is inconceivable and impossible.

127. They are also **SELF-EVIDENT**. All demonstration is derived from them, but they themselves escape demonstration.

128. First truths either govern the moral conduct and establish the absolute difference between good and evil, thus constituting the **PRACTICAL REASON**; or they are the guiding principles of scientific research, thus constituting the **PURE REASON**.

129. The pure reason comprises : (1) **LOGICAL PRIN-
CIPLES** without which thought cannot come to an understanding with itself, — as the principles of identity and contradiction ; (2) **OBJECTIVE PRINCIPLES** without which
science would be impossible, — causation, substance, and
order; (3) the **NOTION OF THE INFINITE.**

130. The origin of the ideas of the reason has been differently explained. The **SENSUALISTS** believe they can
explain it by experience; while the **IDEALISTS** admit,
under different forms, that the reason is **INNATE.**

131. The truths of the reason are innate in this sense, that
they antedate experience as so many natural dispositions ;
but experience is necessary in order to develop and define
them.

CHAPTER XIII

LANGUAGE AND ITS RELATIONS WITH THOUGHT

228. Review of the Intellectual Functions. — We have followed the human intelligence in the different stages of its evolution ; we have seen how the functions of perception collect the elements of intelligence under the direction of the reason, which is the source of the first principle according to which the mind is organized ; how the memory and the representative imagination preserve these elements ; and, finally, how the faculties of elaboration transform them and succeed in building up the human consciousness.

In a word, the reason furnishes, so to speak, the plan of the building ; the senses and the consciousness collect the materials and place them in charge of the memory ; then generalization, abstraction, imagination, and reasoning take hold of them in order to construct the entire edifice.

We would have finished the study of human thought and its laws, if there were not still to be examined the means by which the states of consciousness take shape and become incarnate, so to speak, in the material signs which we call words and which constitute language, and thus are revealed outwardly and are communicated to other men.

229. Language and Thought. — Language, moreover, is not only the necessary instrument for the communication of thought, and hence one of the essential conditions of human society ; but it is also an indispensable auxiliary to thought itself. Thought owes to it a part of its progress. Even without communicating itself, and while enclosed within the circle of the individual consciousness, thought cannot dispense with language. We speak our thought mentally, before speaking it outwardly for the benefit of others. The material representation of words accompanies all our conceptions.

But before explaining the services which language renders thought, it is necessary to define it and to indicate its nature and origin.

230. Definition of Language. — We purpose to speak in this place, neither of the language of physiognomy and gesture, nor of written language and books. This study would carry us away too far. It must suffice to consider spoken language, or speech, which is the most important of all, and one of the essential characteristics of man.

Spoken language may be defined as follows :—*A system of signs by means of which we give outward expression to all our states of consciousness.*

231 Signs. — Signs are sensible facts which represent other facts ; signs are always material, and the thing signified may also be material. For example : lightning is the sign of thunder ; in certain countries the branch of a tree placed over a door signifies the existence of a wine-shop. Or the things signified may be immaterial facts. The words of spoken language signify the invisible thoughts and feelings, which, without language, would remain, as it, were, buried and concealed in the individual consciousness.

232. Natural Signs and Artificial Signs. — Signs are either natural or artificial. In the first case, they are immediately understood because they are derived from nature itself, and the instinct which produced them also interprets them. In the second case, they result from convention, and are consequently intelligible only by those who have learned the value of the arbitrary relation established between them and the things signified.

"There are signs," says Jouffroy,* "which all men use and understand uniformly. The child finds these signs and understands them without having learned them. Artificial signs, on the contrary, result from mere convention, and, this association of the sign with the thing signified being arbitrary, it has nothing of the universal in it."

To the category of natural signs we must refer laughter, or the expression of joy ; tears, which indicate suffering ; and, in general, the gestures and movements of the features which translate the inner passions outwardly, — as blushing, pallor, etc.

As examples of artificial signs, we may note the different systems of writing whose symbols have no relation with the sounds which they express, — such as telegraphic and maritime signals.

As to spoken language, it is a question whether it is a system of natural signs or of artificial signs. Natural in its origin, language has become artificial in its developments and transformations, and the diversity of languages (the number of known languages being not less than nine hundred) is an incontestable proof of this.

233. How the Child learns to speak. — The child learns to speak chiefly through imitation. He repeats, like a parrot, the sounds which he hears pronounced, and attaches to them a meaning, right or wrong, as it may chance to be. If there are deaf-mutes, it is because, deaf from birth, these unfortunates have not been able to reproduce sounds which they have never heard.

Language is then a tradition which the generations transmit to one another, and which is thus maintained across the centuries.

It is important, however, to note that the child, in a certain sense, invents language: that he displays marked activity in the acquisition of the mother-tongue; and that in his earliest years he manifests a real spontaneity in the use of words.

All observers have noticed this initiative of the child.

"Nothing is more admirable," says Renan,* "than

the child's power of expression, and the ingenuity
which he displays in creating a language of his own
before the traditional language has been imposed on
him."

I am well aware that many words in the child's language have been dictated to him by his nurse and his
mother, who repeat in his ear the phrases of the traditional language of infancy. The words of correct
speech are expressly disfigured in order to render them
more intelligible. On the other hand, certain expressions in the child's vocabulary, apparently original, are
due wholly to his awkwardness in repeating the sounds
which he hears.

But, with these reservations, something is still due to
the inventive activity of the child.

" The child," says Albert Lemoine, "has more to do
than we think with the language which we teach him.
He is the inventor of half of it, though we fancy we
give it to him ready made. See him when the organ of
speech, still obstructed, does not obey his feeble will;
even then he is capable of modulating some vowels, and
articulating some consonants formed at random, by the
ill-directed movements of his lips and tongue. . . .
You fancy that it is really his mother who teaches him
the first articulate sign, the first word having a meaning.
Undeceive yourselves ; it is the child who gives the
first lesson, and it is the mother who learns it. The
first word which he pronounces, and to which he at-

taches a meaning, is not a word of the mother-tongue which he learns from his nurse, but it is he who coins it out of formless matter, it is he who attaches to it a meaning; it is a word of his own language, and his nurse learns this language from him before she teaches him her own. This language of the child, very poor, whose vocabulary is composed of a few sounds, of modulated cries, and of syllables scarcely articulated, — this is the instrument which his mother will use in order to make him comprehend and accept the scholarly language of his country and his century." [1]

The child then co-operates actively in the acquisition of language ; and it is not merely in the invention of words that he manifests this spontaneity, but also in the natural logic of his grammar. "The child's language," says Max Müller,* an authority on this subject, "is more regular than our own. If children had had their way, they would little by little have eliminated a great number of irregular forms." [2]

234. Origin of Language. — If it is true that a child invents his language in part, it is none the less certain that humanity has invented languages complete in all their parts. No one to-day would think of reviving the old theory which, declaring man incapable of inventing a single word, asserted that he had originally received from God, through direct revelation and tradition, a primitive language completely formed.

---

[1] Albert Lemoine, *De la Physionomie et de la Parole*, p. 149.
[2] Max Müller, *Lectures on the Science of Language.*

No : languages have a natural origin. Incessantly
modified by men in the course of time, they were also
at their first appearance created by men.

"It is a dream," says Renan, "to imagine a primitive
state when man did not speak, followed by another
state when he understood the use of speech. It is as
natural for man to speak as it is to think ; and it is as
little philosophic to assign a definite beginning to language as to thought."

It is now the almost unanimous belief, that the first
words used by men were natural cries or interjections,
which were taken as signs, either of the inner emotions
which they expressed, or of the exterior objects which
provoked these emotions ; for example, the sounds and
noises observed in nature, as the note of a bird, the cry
of an animal, or the noise of thunder. The primitive
roots of languages are either interjections or onomato-
pœas * (imitations of the sounds of nature).

235. Can we think without Language? — The services
which language renders thought are so considerable
that through an unwarrantable exaggeration it has been
affirmed that language is the very condition of thought.
This has been expressed by de Bonald * in this aphorism :
" Man thinks his speech before he speaks his thought."
Speech, in other terms, is prior to thought. Man
thinks only by means of signs.

Facts disprove this theory. Deaf-mutes think, although they have not the use of speech. It is true they

employ other signs than words; but they could not appropriate these signs if they did not previously have thoughts.

The child would never learn to speak if he did not already have ideas. He is qualified to retain words, only because he grasps the relation that connects them with the thoughts which they express.

Doubtless, in the adult, such an indissoluble cohesion has taken place between the idea and the word, that we scarcely have an idea which is not accompanied by a word. Even in our purely inward reflections, we mentally pronounce the words which are the symbols of our ideas. But, if words are the instruments of thought, they certainly do not create thought. We perceive material things, we experience mental anguish, we recall our past states, we even judge and reason, without the aid of words. An unknown object strikes my eyes; I do not know its name, but yet I perceive this object. Two different colors present themselves to my notice; I do not need to think of their names in order to judge that they are different.

To a certain degree, then, thought is independent of words. An additional proof of this is the disproportion which sometimes exists between the power of thought and the gift of speech. Doubtless it is usually true to say with Boileau : —

"What is well conceived is clearly expressed."

It sometimes happens, however, that even profound

thinkers are not eloquent ; they experience great embarrassment in giving outward expression to their
thought.

It is in the case of particular and sensible items of
knowledge that thought needs the aid of words the
least. The intelligence, which always seeks a material
basis of support, finds it, in this case, in the objects
themselves. On the contrary, when the thought rises
to abstract and general ideas, the intervention of words
becomes more necessary, because words are then the
only material thing on which thought can fix itself.

236. The Services which Language renders Thought. —
But when we have proved that thought precedes language, and that we are capable of speaking only because we are capable of thinking, we must hasten to
add that, without language, thought would be singularly
impotent. In truth, in the actual state of things,
thought being constantly united with speech, it is difficult for us to judge to what point of intellectual feeble-
ness the privation of language would sink us. We
may, however, indicate from what special points of view
language is the indispensable instrument of thought.
It is (1) an instrument of analysis ; (2) an instrument
of precision ; (3) a mnemotechnic instrument ; (4) an
instrument of abbreviation.

237. Language an Instrument of Analysis. — Condillac
said that languages are *analytical methods*. Doubtless
the analysis of thought is pre-eminently an inward

operation, an intellectual process; and if the mechanism of language does not accomplish the analysis, it at
least facilitates it. Moreover, certain judgments are in
some degree instantaneous acts of the mind; and language can express them only successively and by different words. Each of these words is, for each element
of thought, something analogous to the little receivers
in which the chemist, after having decomposed a body,
puts apart the various simple elements resulting from
this decomposition. And so, having separated one from
another the different parts of its judgments, and having
immobilized them, so to speak, in distinct words, the
mind is in a better condition to compare them and to
grasp their relations.

238. Language an Instrument of Precision. — Everybody knows how vague and uncertain our thoughts
remain as long as they have not been expressed. Our
conceptions are confused until they have found their
verbal form. How many times has it happened to us
to attribute great value to conceptions which, when
translated into words, seem to us feeble and without
import! Words are the pitiless translators of our
thoughts; and they bring to the light all their faults.
In return, they alone give to our ideas all their potency
and all their clearness.

239. Language an Aid to Memory. — Language is
also a *mnemotechnic** instrument, and this advantage
really results from the preceding statements. In fact,

it is precisely because it facilitates the analysis of thought, and also because it fixes ideas by incorporating them into words, that language assists the memory. It is impossible to conceive what the memory would be without the aid of language, — a sort of confused chaos where we would walk by feeling our way. By means of words, on the contrary, we easily manage our recollec- tions, especially when these recollections are applied to general ideas.

" A word suffices to represent to us the result to which we have been led by long and painful operations. It is a total which has been given us by a toilsome series of partial additions. Withdraw this word, that is to say, this sum, and you condemn yourself to pass over the same routes the second time, to recommence the same toil. . . . Language, by associating ideas with words, fixes and solidifies them. By means of language, abstraction and generalization, though pure conceptions, assume form and substance, and thus live an independ- ent existence, which, wholly fortuitous though it be, nevertheless permits us to hold them in reserve and to recover them at need."[1]

240. Language an Instrument of Abbreviation. — Finally, language is also useful and necessary because it simpli- fies and abridges the labor of thought. When ideas present themselves to the mind, they are always accom- panied, to a greater or less degree, by images. If we think of a valley, however rapid our thought may be,

[1] Albert Lemoine, *op. cit.*

our imagination represents to us at once meadows, forests, and neighboring mountains. If we think of humanity, even this abstract idea brings with it a train of images, as the representation of such a man or of such a race. And so, through the intervention of words, this labor of imaginative representation is spared the mind. The word is substituted, in part, for the images ; it becomes, for the disciplined mind, the equivalent of the idea ; so that we think with words and no longer with ideas. When we read or pronounce a discourse, we certainly have not the time to conceive, back of each word, all that the word signifies. Just as algebraic signs aid the mathematician in his calculations, because they substitute more abstract signs, or conventional symbols, for real and determinate numbers ; so words become a substitute for thought and save us a useless labor.

It is true that the advantages of language encounter inconveniences and dangers at this point. In fact, we are exposed to the danger of forgetting things and ideas themselves, and of relying too much upon words ; and, instead of reflecting on the relations which exist between signs and the thing signified, our thought sometimes becomes purely verbal. The danger of " realized abstractions " is also true of language.

But, notwithstanding, language forms, in some degree, an integral part of thought. Created by thought, it in turn develops it, aids it, and defines it ; finally, it lightens the burden of the intelligence.

SUMMARY.

132. Spoken **LANGUAGE** is not merely the necessary **INSTRUMENT** for the communication of thought; but is an **AUXILIARY** in the inner development of individual thought.

133. Language is a **COLLECTION OF SIGNS** by means of which we give outward expression to our states of consciousness.

134. Signs are always material facts.

135. There are two categories of signs: **NATURAL SIGNS**, which are universal and immediately intelligible; and **ARTIFICIAL SIGNS**, which express only a conventional relation, and consequently need to be learned.

136. Language, **NATURAL IN ITS ORIGIN**, has become **ARTIFICIAL IN ITS DEVELOPMENT AND TRANSFORMATIONS.**

137. The child learns to speak chiefly through **IMITATION**; he nevertheless evinces a real spontaneity in the acquisition of language.

138. In its origin, language borrowed its first vocal elements, either from interjections, or from the **CRIES OF ANIMALS** and **NOISES IN NATURE.**

139. It has been asserted, though incorrectly, that speech preceded **THOUGHT**. Thought is certainly **PRIOR TO LANGUAGE**, but it cannot dispense with it.

140. In reality, language renders eminent services to thought. It is an **INSTRUMENT OF ANALYSIS**, since it permits us to decompose the various elements of thought by connecting them with distinct words.

141. It is an **INSTRUMENT OF PRECISION,** for it gives definite form to our conceptions.

142. It is a **MNEMOTECHNIC INSTRUMENT**; for it fixes and consolidates, so to speak, the acquired results of our intellectual operations.

143. Finally, it is an **INSTRUMENT OF ABBREVIA-TION**; for it simplifies the labor of thought, and renders the mind services analogous to those which algebra renders the science of numbers.

CHAPTER XIV

MORAL SENSIBILITY. PERSONAL INCLINATIONS

241. Moral Sensibility. — We have studied (Chapter III.) the physical sensibility and the sensations; but have postponed the examination of the *moral sensibility* and the *feelings*, till after the study of the intelligence. The feelings, in fact, presuppose all the previous ideas and conceptions. The moral sensibility is the sensibility vivified by the intelligence, and guided and directed by it towards objects superior to the senses and to the organic functions. Feeling has always an idea for its point of support. The selfish feelings suppose the idea of self; the affectionate feelings, the idea of the persons whom we love and of their qualities; patriotism corresponds to the idea of native country.

242. The Functions of Sensibility. — There have been philosophers who decry sensibility. The Stoics * wished to exclude feeling from the life of the sage. The perfect man, in their eyes, was the insensible man, indifferent to the death of his parents and friends, and to the ruin of his country.

Good sense does justice to these chimeras. To tell the truth, man is the more perfect as he is the better endowed with feeling; on condition, however, that his sensibility is regulated by reason, that it does not degenerate into sentimentality, and that it does not go astray in the excesses of passion.

The pleasures which result from the moral sensibility, — the pleasures of affection, of art, and of science, — far from being unworthy of man, are perhaps the noblest part of his nature.

Besides rendering life agreeable, they have their intrinsic excellence ; they are proofs, as much as the reason is, of the dignity of our nature.

Moreover, the emotions of the sensibility exercise a profound influence over the other faculties.

The intelligence is doubtless sometimes disturbed by the sensibility, and the mind may become the dupe of the heart. But in other cases, on the contrary, the intellectual faculties are animated and powerfully excited by feeling. It is not without reason that Vauvenargues * has said : " The great thoughts come from the heart."

The will would most often be powerless if it also were not sustained by feeling. It does not suffice to will the good ; it must be loved. Grand actions and heroic sacrifices are almost always inspired by feeling. The inclinations have a high rank among the very principles of the moral life and voluntary activity. Certain austere moralists, like Kant, are wrong in proscribing pleasure from ethics. Schiller,* while bantering these modern stoics, said with a smile : " I feel remorse, and

begin to feel myself a culprit ; I take pleasure in oblig-
ing my friends." The pleasure felt in being virtuous
never mars the virtue of which it is the reward.

Suffering itself has its part in human life, and Alfred
de Musset,* a great poet, could say with reason :

"Man is an apprentice ; and sorrow is his master."

Suffering is a stimulant, for it excites us to struggle
against it, and to use all our efforts to relieve ourselves
from its embrace. It is also a tonic, for it fortifies the
character.

243. The Inclinations. — The moral sensibility comprises a great number of tendencies to which we give
the general name of *inclinations*.

Inclination, then, is a natural tendency which has an
idea or a conception for a point of departure, and which,
when it is satisfied, gives rise to a feeling of joy, but
when it is opposed, to a feeling of sorrow.

Every inclination for an object supposes a contrary
aversion. The love of the beautiful corresponds to an
aversion for the ugly ; the love of riches, to a repulsion
for poverty.

244. Different Forms of Inclination. — Inclination, according as its object is present or absent, past or to come,
easy or difficult to attain, traverses different periods or
stages which give rise to particular states of the mind.

If the object of the inclination is present, the mind,
as Bossuet said, enjoys its felicity and reposes in it.
The inclination then takes the form of *joy*.

If, on the contrary, the object is absent; if we are deprived of it, and if, instead of the good, a corresponding evil is realized ; our soul suffers, and this is *sadness*.

When the good pursued by our inclination is something future, we await it with impatience and solicit it with all our heart.   This is *desire*.

If circumstances seem to us to render some future good probable, we count on a .oming pleasure; and this is *hope*.

" Desire," said Bossuet, " is a passion which impels us to seek what we love when it is absent."   And again, " Desire is a love which reaches out for a good which it does not have.   Hope is a love which flatters itself that it will possess the object loved."

If it is the evil which is awaited, and not the good, we experience *fear* instead of *hope*.

If the object of our inclination is past, we experience a peculiar sadness which is called *regret*.

If all sorts of difficulties keep us away from the object loved, we become irritated at these obstacles; and this is *anger*.

All these modifications of inclination depend simply on circumstances ; they constitute the modes or forms which every inclination may assume.

Thus the patriot rejoices in the success of his country.   He is sad if his country is conquered and humiliated.   He desires to see her rise again in the future. When she is engaged in a military expedition, or in diplomatic negotiations, he hopes and fears for her in turn. Sometimes he looks back upon her past glories with regret. The ambitious man, the miser, — every man, in a word, who is possessed by an inclination, passes in succession through these different states.

245. Classification of the Passions according to Bossuet. — Bossuet improperly called these different states of the sensibility, *passions.* " Passion," he says, " is the movement of the soul which, touched with the pleasure or the pain felt or imagined in an object, pursues it or shrinks from it."

He enumerated eleven passions : love and hate, desire and aversion, joy and sorrow, boldness and fear, hope and despair, and lastly, anger.

And he further remarked that all these passions "are connected with one love which restrains or excites them all. . . . Take away love, and there is no longer passion ; add love, and you produce them all." All the other passions, shame, envy, emulation, admiration, astonishment, and some others like them, are, according to him, but modifications of the eleven primitive passions.

246. Criticism of this Theory. — It is no longer customary to employ the word "passion " to designate the different forms of inclination. It was through a singular abuse of language that Bossuet applied this term, the synonym of a violent state of ardent emotion, to a feeling as calm and as mild as hope. Moreover, in his incomplete theory, Bossuet did not take into account the circumstance that the object of our inclination is often in the past, and that from this circumstance there result new modifications in the form of the inclination. Finally, it was arbitrary for Bossuet to count eleven passions and no more. It is impossible for the most exact psychology to enumerate with such precision the different changes and movements of love, by reason of the complex elements which are ever introducing variations into its manifestations.

247. True Characteristics of Passion. — As it seems to us, we must reserve the word "passions" to designate the extreme states of every inclination. Generally moderate at its beginning, associating itself in the soul with a host of other inclinations which share among themselves our faculty of loving, each inclination tends to exalt itself, to become exclusive and jealous, to monopolize all our thoughts, and to aim at sole domination.

Passion is violent and impetuous : it enslaves our will and obscures our intelligence. It throws disorder into the soul. It is most often evil and vicious. It may be defined as inordinate and perverted sensibility.

All our inclinations, even the highest, under the influence of circumstances, become exaggerated and corrupted. It is not only the personal inclinations which give rise to passions such as intemperance, avarice, and culpable ambition ; but even the purest and the noblest feelings may degenerate through excess into feelings that are evil or to be regretted. Excess of religious feeling leads to fanaticism; excess of the patriotic feeling may inspire a fierce hatred of the foreigner; excess of paternal or maternal feeling may engender mischievous partiality and unjustifiable preferences.

248. Different Kinds of Inclinations. — We have not only to distinguish the forms of inclination, but also to divide them into certain classes according to the ends which they pursue. There will be as many kinds of *inclinations* as there are distinct objects to which our conscious sensibility may attach its affection.

249. Division of Inclinations. — The division of inclinations into kinds is therefore founded on the difference among the objects to which they relate.

Sometimes we love ourselves, and self is the source of our emotions and feelings. Hence arise the *personal* or *selfish inclinations*.

Or we love other men, our companions, our parents, our fellow-citizens, or our friends. These are the *social inclinations*, or affectionate feelings which are summed up in the love of others, and which the positivist school designates by the term *altruistic inclinations*.

And, finally, our sensibility passes beyond persons, and attaches itself to the ideas and conceptions of our mind, as the beautiful, the true, and the good. These are the *ideal inclinations*, and they might also be called the impersonal feelings.

250. Personal Inclinations. — The common principle of all the personal inclinations is the *love of self*, which is itself but the consequence of a more general inclination, the *love of existence*. From the simple fact that we exist, we tend to persevere in existence, and we love whatever contributes towards increasing, or at least preserving, our existence. Hence arise, according to the very diversity of the things which contribute to the development of life, the particular inclinations which are connected with the different forms of existence.

251. The Instinct of Conservation. — The first manifestation of the love of self is the *instinct of conservation*, the love of life. The most unhappy men prefer life to death :

> " Rather suffer than die,
> Is the motto of men."

It is true that this motto is sometimes disproved by facts, and that suicide contradicts it. In this case it is a stronger inclination which triumphs over the instinct of conservation. He who voluntarily cuts short his days loves life as well as other men do ; but this love of life is swayed, in his case, by a violent passion which bears down with a heavier weight in the balance of his resolutions. The fear of physical suffering and the sense of moral pain have, in the case of the suicide, gained ascendency over every other consideration.

252. Self-Love. — One of the most characteristic forms of the instinct of conservation is *self-love*, which is derived not merely from the love of existence, but from the love of perfection. We wish not only to exist, but to excel in everything, to distinguish ourselves from our fellows and to be their superiors. From self-love are derived a great number of feelings, good and bad.

Legitimate in its origin, self-love tends, in fact, to degenerate through excess. It is right to esteem one's self, to have a good opinion of self, but yet on one condition ; and this is that we merit this esteem and this good opinion. Now, through partiality for ourselves, we are disposed not only to exaggerate the worth of the virtues which we possess, but to ascribe to ourselves virtues which we do not have, and to conceal from ourselves our most striking faults.

Self-love also leads us to plume ourselves on vain and insignificant advantages ; it then becomes *vanity*, while *pride*, though equally censurable, is derived from an exaggerated consciousness of qualities which have their value. To boast of a beautiful face or a fine dress, is vanity ; while to show off or feel conceited because one is eloquent or wise, is pride.

Self-love gives rise to a multitude of feelings, as the love of praise, of approbation, of esteem, love of glory, emulation, etc., — feelings, we repeat, which are legitimate in themselves, but which are easily perverted and so become false ; emulation, for example, becomes transformed into jealousy.

253. Love of Power. — *Love of power*, or ambition, is

a derivative from the love of self. Some men seek power because power permits their activity to display itself freely; because, moreover, it brings them into personal prominence and draws to themselves at least the apparent respect of other men ; and, finally, because it assures to them a preponderance or domination among their fellows.

" The imperious character becomes noticeable even in infancy. Notice children in their plays. There is one among them who is their general if they form an army, and their coachman if it is an equipage. Alcibiades * gave an early proof of his love of domination. While still very young he was playing at huckle-bones in a narrow street. As it was his turn to throw them, he saw a loaded cart approaching. He at once shouted to the driver to stop. As the man continued to advance, the other children retired ; but Alcibiades, throwing himself on the ground before the horses, said to the driver: 'Come on now if you will!' . . . We know nothing of the childhood of Napoleon, except that at Brienne, when his companions in their play had built fortresses of snow, it was he who led the attack." [1]

The love of power is not so much the love of power for its own sake, as the love of the consequences which result from it. Ambition is the trait of an encroaching personality which aspires to make his will absolute, to dominate, if not to destroy, the wills of others.

Ambition, while it measures its strength with the

[1] Garnier, *Traité des facultés de l'âme*, t. iv., p 171.

real powers of an individual, and, to attain its end,
uses only allowable means, is a legitimate inclination.
There are noble and beautiful ambitions; but too often
the love of power betrays aims disproportionate to the
merit of the ambitious man; and, consequently, like
all the passions, it may lead men on to culpable and
criminal acts.

254. The Love of Property. — Property being a condition of personal well-being, an element of happiness, it
is just to count among the selfish inclinations the *love
of property.* " What is my own is near to me; the
things which belong to us are like an extension of our
personality." [1]

The love of property is already noticeable in the
child, who early defends his toys, his copy-books, and
his books, against every attempt at usurpation. But it
holds a very large place in the preoccupations of the
mature man; and then it readily tends towards exaggeration, towards becoming a mania, a vice, *avarice.*

"There are men who accumulate for the simple
pleasure of accumulating. Some accumulate a multitude of incongruous objects which can never be of any
use to them; others, far from desiring any advantage
from the supplies they have accumulated, see in them
no other utility than the accumulation itself; they are
unwilling to part with the fruits of their store-room,
with the wine of their cellar, or with the coin in their
cash-box; they receive their revenues only to refund

[1] Garnier, *op. cit.,* t. iv., p. 171.

them, and to collect new proceeds which they again invest ; they are in despair at the idea that all this must be given up, and that men go stripped to the tomb. . . . A miser often loves his money better than he does his children. Molière's *Harpagon* * is a proof of this. . . . The miser, says Pope, is as much a slave as the negro employed in the mines. The only difference between them is that one unearths gold, and the other buries it." [1]

255. Selfishness. — All the manifestations of self-love, when they exceed moderation, are summed up in *selfishness*, that is, the moral state of the man who connects everything with himself, with his own personal interests.

To think of self, to prefer self to all others, is a primitive instinct, contemporary with the first awakening of consciousness. The love of liberty, the love of nature, and still other feelings, suppose a certain progress in reflection. Man does not become a patriot or a philanthropist, save as he is educated ; but he is selfish simply because he is a man. Doubtless our actual social condition is of a nature to develop selfishness, by reason of the increase in independence and well-being ; but, on the other hand, the effect of civilization is more and more to strengthen the benevolent and social feelings, and consequently to reduce the amount of selfishness in our hearts.

"Civilization," says August Comte,* "by developing to an immense and always increasing degree the action

1 Garnier, *op. cit.*, t. i., p. 132.

of man on the external world, . . . civilization seems at first destined to concentrate our attention more and more on the cares of our mere material existence, whose maintenance and amelioration constitute, apparently, the principal object of most social occupations ; but a more profound examination shows, on the contrary, that this development tends continually to give precedence to the higher faculties of human nature (the generous sentiments), either by the very security which it necessarily inspires with respect to physical needs whose consideration becomes less and less absorbing ; or by the direct and continuous excitation which it necessarily impresses on the intellectual functions and even on the social feelings." [1]

256. Evil Consequences of Selfishness. — Moralists have often described the caprices of selfishness.

"Gnathon," says La Bruyère, "knows no other misfortunes than his own. He does not weep over the death of others ; he apprehends only his own, which he would willingly redeem by the extinction of the human race. . . . Gnathon lives only for himself, and all the men in the world are, in his sight, as though they did not exist."

We might perhaps call in question the second part of the aphorism. The egoist knows that there are men, and he makes use of them.

Pascal says, to the same effect : —

" The *me* is odious because it is unjust, because it

---

[1] August Comte, *Philosophie positive.*

makes itself the centre of everything. The 'me' is disagreeable to others because it wishes to domineer over them. Each 'me' is the enemy and would be the tyrant of all others. We must detest it because it declares itself openly, or because it dissembles itself through politeness and in order not to cause displeasure to others."

It is worthy of special remark that the egoist deceives himself and is his own dupe. He seeks nothing but happiness, but has taken the wrong road to find it. Doubtless he does not suffer over the misfortunes of others, since he does not love others. Fielding has wittily said that the selfishness which coils a man up like a ball makes him capable of rolling along in the world without ever being affected by the misfortunes of others.

But precisely because he has concentrated all his affections on himself, the egoist will find in his personal misfortunes, — deceptions of his vanity, wounds to his pride, accidents to health, and vicissitudes of fortune, — sources of bitterness whose violence nothing will ever correct or assuage, since he has excluded himself from every other source of happiness. The egoist is thus a blunderer and is lacking as much in spirit as in heart. He has made a false calculation in his passionate search for happiness. It is in the generous affections, and in devotion to others, that the secret of happiness resides. Let us then exert ourselves to become detached from ourselves.   Let us recollect that the sweetest of our joys are even those which we procure for others.

"It is by bringing the coals together that they burn," says the Indian proverb. So it is the union of men that gives them their power and their happiness; and like the coals, also, it is by separating themselves that they lose their warmth and vitality. The good things of this world are sweeter when shared with others than when enjoyed alone; and as a fabulist has said:

"The whole is not worth the half."

Saint Theresa, wishing to show that the real merit of men resides in charity, said: "At death we no longer possess anything; there remains nothing save what we have given away."

And so, true personal happiness consists in loving others. The "me" is really satisfied only when it has been absorbed in others. It is never happier than when it has forgotten itself. The true selfishness consists in not being selfish.

SUMMARY.

144. The **MORAL SENSIBILITY** is the sensibility vivified and directed by the intelligence.

145. The facts of moral sensibility have received the generic name of **FEELINGS**. Every feeling supposes an object known by the intelligence, and, consequently, an idea, — the idea of what is loved.

146. The sensibility plays an important and useful part in human life. It not only renders existence agreeable and charming, but the feelings have their own proper excellence and dignity; moreover, they excite thought and stimulate action.

147. The feelings are derived from a certain number of natural tendencies called **INCLINATIONS**

148. Every inclination assumes different **FORMS** according as the object which it pursues is present or absent, past or future, easy or difficult to attain.

149. Bossuet was wrong in calling the forms and modes of inclination **PASSIONS.** Passion is an extreme, violent, and excessive state of the inclinations.

150. The inclinations may be distributed into a certain number of **SPECIES**, according to the difference in the objects to which they are attached.

151. There are three species of inclinations: the **PERSONAL** inclinations, the **SOCIAL** or affectionate inclinations, and the **IDEAL** inclinations.

152. The source of the personal inclinations is the **LOVE OF SELF**, which is itself derived from the love of existence.

153. The different manifestations of the love of self are the **INSTINCT OF CONSERVATION, SELF-LOVE, LOVE OF POWER**, and the **LOVE OF PROPERTY**.

154. Legitimate in their origin, the seinclinations tend to become exaggerated, exclusive, and, consequently, evil.

155. We call **SELFISHNESS** the moral state of a man in whom the personal inclinations have an exclusive domination.

CHAPTER XV

THE SOCIAL INCLINATIONS AND THE IDEAL
INCLINATIONS

257. The Social Inclinations. — The common characteristic of the personal inclinations is that they are
interested. Having self for their object, they seek personal good ; they are governed by interest.

The *social inclinations*, on the contrary, are disinterested ; they tend to the good of others. They all consist in disengaging a person from himself, in forgetting
his own happiness in order to seek the happiness of
others.

258. Improper Use of the Word Love. — It is for the
social inclinations, consequently, that must be reserved
the beautiful word "love," which ordinary language
strangely misuses. It is customary to say that one
loves himself, and that the glutton loves wine and
coffee. But what relation is there between these selfish and inferior feelings and the generous emotions
which attach us to others, and which make our hearts
beat for our country and for justice ? Doubtless pleasure accompanies all our sensations and all our feelings,
and it is for this reason that language has sanctioned
the custom of saying that we love all the things that

procure us pleasure. But there is no comparison possible between the material enjoyments of the senses
and the noble joys of affection under all its forms. He
alone loves truly, who, renouncing self, bestows upon
others the glowing emotions of his heart.

259. Division of the Social Inclinations. — In the first
place, we love all men in general, and this is *sociability ;*
in the second place, we love more particularly, among
men, those who are the most nearly related to us, those
who are united to us by ties of blood, — these are
the *family affections ;* in the third place, we consecrate
a particular affection to our country and to our fellow-
citizens, — these are the *patriotic feelings ;* and finally,
we experience feelings of individual affection for the
persons whom we prefer to all others, and who become
the objects of an exclusive and privileged tenderness, —
these are *love* and *friendship.*

260. Sophism of Rousseau. — Sociability is a universal
inclination, to which no man of a sound mind is a
stranger. Misanthropes are monstrous exceptions.
Every man, in the normal conditions of his moral
development, loves humanity. Savage tribes themselves
are societies, imperfect and rudimentary, doubtless, but
even in them individuals find pleasure in aiding one
another. The child who does not yet know what the
family is, testifies his joy at the sight of human faces.

Nevertheless, the existence of the social instinct has
been called in question. Rousseau, always ready with

a sophism,* has asserted that society is but a natural fact. Hobbes * had previously maintained the same opinion.

" Nature," says Rousseau, " has taken but little pains to bring men together ; she has made but little prepara- tion for their sociability. . . . It is impossible to imag- ine why, in a primitive state, a man should have more need of another man, than a monkey or a wolf, of one of its kind. Society does not necessarily result from the faculties of man, and could not have been estab- lished save by the aid of hazard, and by circumstances that might not have taken place."

So, then, social life is but a hazard, an accident. Aristotle had replied in advance to the paradoxes of Rousseau, when he defined man "a social animal," and when he added : —

" Men are united because they could not support themselves in isolation, although the pleasure of living together was of itself capable of founding society."

It is hardly necessary to say more in refutation of Rousseau's opinion. The universal fact of the exist- ence of societies gives it a formal contradiction. Man would be powerless to develop himself physically and morally if he lived alone. The natural faculty of lan- guage would no longer have reason for existence outside of society.

But what we are aiming particularly to prove is not that society is a natural and necessary fact, but that it is a source of pleasure, and that a common feeling of affection unites us to all men.

261. Need of Sociability. — The social inclination, being one of those which are the most constantly satisfied, does not give rise to enjoyments as keen as the inclinations which enter into possession of their object only rarely and at long intervals. Pleasure, in other words, is not a durable state. By prolonging itself it becomes extinguished.

But let some circumstance come to deprive us of the society of our fellows, and then we shall feel a discomfort which, by its very keenness, will give evidence of the secret and concealed power of the feeling whose sweetness long habit has hidden from us.

Robinson Crusoe * was conceived by the English novelist to prove that, in a certain measure, the individual, by his labor and personal industry, may supply the place of the social co-operation of all men. Yet Robinson Crusoe himself admits that there is at least one thing which he keenly misses, and this is the companionship of his fellows ; and it is this which renders his exclamations so touching, when, after having vainly searched the ruins of the stranded boat, he cries : —

" Ah ! if a man had been saved ! If a single man could have been saved ! "

Silvio Pellico * relates, in the memoirs of his captivity, how he was gladdened at the sight of a man, were that man a jailer : " I went to the window longing for the

sight of some new face, and I thought myself happy if
the sentinel in his rounds did not graze the wall in
passing, but kept far enough from it so that it might be
possible for me to see him. When the soldier, who had
a face expressing honesty, raised his head, and when I
thought I could discover in it some trace of compassion,
I experienced a gentle palpitation, as if this unknown
soldier had been my friend. When he withdrew, I
awaited his return with a tender anxiety, and if he
looked at me as he came back, I rejoiced at it as a great
act of charity."

It is not only in prison that there springs up this
melancholy of solitude, this pining for society. Franklin * relates how, on the open sea, in a voyage which had
lasted for a long time, the meeting with a vessel was
for the passengers a real merry-making : he goes on to
say that on one of his voyages he fell in with a vessel
sailing from Dublin to New York, having fifty laborers
of both sexes. They all appeared on deck and seemed
transported with joy at the sight of another vessel. ` To
meet a vessel on the open sea causes a real gratification.
We love to see again creatures of our own species after
having been separated for a long time from the rest of
mankind. My heart beat with joy, he adds, and I
laughed with delight. The two captains promised to
continue their voyage in company, but shortly afterward the *Neige* was lost from sight, and sadness once
more invaded the whole company.

262. Sympathy. — The social inclinations, under all their forms, are sometimes called *sympathetic*, because they have their common source in sympathy. The love of other men in general, the love of our parents, friendship, — in a word, all the affections, suppose that we sympathize with the persons who are the objects of our love.

But sympathy is to be understood in two different senses. First, it is simply the tendency on our part to put our feelings in accord with those of others. We laugh with those who laugh, we weep with those who weep. In a crowd at the theatre we easily participate in the emotions experienced by our fellows. But sympathy is something besides this ; it is the tendency to love those who have the same feelings that we have, those who have some resemblance with our own nature. . . . And the second form of sympathy, as we know, is but the consequence of the first. In fact, our affections extend themselves by preference to those who most resemble us in their character, in their virtues, or in their faults. It is the law of resemblance which guides the affections and the unions of the heart, just as we have already seen that it directs a great number of our intellectual associations. We love all men, because, in a general way, they resemble us ; we love our parents and our fellow-citizens more, because they resemble us in a more particular way ; finally, we prefer our friends to other men, because there is between them and us a greater community of opinions, manners, and habits.

263. Refutation of La Rochefoucauld. — If, as a practical fact, there are egoists who, denying all disinterested affection, reserve for themselves all their sensibility, there are also, theoretically, moralists and philosophers who deny to man the power of truly loving other men. This is the thesis, for example, of the author of the *Maximes*, La Rochefoucauld.* According to him, the love of self and the things of self is the common basis and the unique source of all our inclinations, even of those which are apparently the most generous and the most disinterested. It is not others whom we really love, it is ourselves whom we love in others; it is the pleasure which others procure for us or the advantages which we expect from others.

"Gratitude," says the author of the *Maximes*, "is like the good faith of merchants, — it maintains commerce. Pity is a skilful prevision of the evils into which we may fall ; services which we render to others are, properly speaking, the good which we do to ourselves in advance. The most disinterested friendship is nothing but a trade in which our self-love always proposes something to be gained. Generosity is but a disguised ambition which spurns a low rate of interest in order to reach a higher. Goodness is indolence or impotence ; or rather, we lend at a high rate of interest under pretext of giving."

If La Rochefoucauld had been content to say that human feelings are often disinterested only in appearance, and that selfishness loves to put on the mask of self-devotion, we might say that he had overdone the strokes of his satire and that he had taken delight in slander and in the portraiture of evil. But he has chosen to generalize, and to establish as a universal rule what is nothing more than an exception ; he has calumniated human nature.

La Rochefoucauld refutes himself, in fact, when he tells us that the disinterested feelings are but feigning hypocrites. He forgets that, in order that there may be simulation in certain cases, there must be reality in other cases. The egoists have an interest in appearing grateful, and they are able by their false protestations to delude those whom they dupe, only because, on the other hand, there are men who are really grateful.

It is true that pleasure always accompanies our emotions, even the most disinterested. The man who forgets himself in order to devote himself to a friend, finds in his devotion an extreme joy and satisfaction. But this pleasure, which is the consequence of the affection, is neither its purpose nor its cause. It is because we love our parents that we find pleasure in loving them ; but it is not the pleasure which is the reason of our love. This is so true, that pleasure can result only from a true and sincere love. "Yes," says Janet, "to love is a pleasure, but it is on the condition of loving, that is, of attaching ourselves to something different from self. If we think of ourselves, the pleasure disappears, the charm is broken."

264. Family Affection. — La Rochefoucauld, whose cynical analysis attacks almost all the feelings, has, nevertheless, respected family affection; he has not dared to say that a mother obeys interested calculations when she devotes herself to her child.

Family affection is one of the most intense and penetrating of the feelings. In ardor of tenderness and energy of devotion, nothing surpasses maternal and paternal affection.

Family affection is also to be regarded as one of the most natural of the feelings, though it is to be recollected that civilization has contributed towards fortifying and refining it, since it has established the foundations of the family on more equitable bases. Formerly, under a *régime* which sanctioned primogenitureship, fraternal affection could not resemble what it is to-day. So also conjugal affection was very different from what it has become, when the wife was not the equal, but the slave, of man.

The affection of parents for children, and of children for parents, has also varied with the progressive tempering of the domestic relations. But this affection has always existed with the peculiar characteristic imposed on it by the manners of the times. Two thousand years ago, Socrates said to his son Lamprocles : " Do

you not owe gratitude to a mother who is so benevolent to you, who, when you are ill, takes care of you to
the utmost of her power that you may recover your
health, and that you may want nothing that is necessary for you, and who, besides, entreats the gods for
many blessings on your head and pays vows for you, —
do you not owe gratitude to such a mother? You,
therefore, my son, if you are wise, will entreat the gods
to pardon you if you have been wanting in respect
towards your mother, lest, regarding you as an ungrateful person, they should be disinclined to do you
good ; and you will have regard, also, to the opinion of
men, lest, observing you to be neglectful of your
parents, they should all condemn you, and you should
then be found destitute of friends; for if men surmise
that you are ungrateful toward your parents, no one
will believe that if he does you a kindness he will meet
with gratitude in return." [1]

265. Patriotism. — Between the love of humanity and
the love of family comes patriotism, more definite and
more restricted than the first, broader and more diffused
than the second.   Different elements contribute to
this, but chiefly the idea of native land, that is, of the
ideal created in our mind either by the conception of
the history of our country, or the thought of our fellow-citizens speaking the same language and united
with us by common interests, or by the representation
of the soil and territory which we inhabit.

[1] Xenophon, *Memorabilia*, book ii., ch. ii.

266. Friendship. — The social affections of which we have thus far been speaking are derived from nature itself. It does not depend upon us to belong to another family or to another country. We do not choose them. But we do choose our friends ; and hence the expression *elective** affinities or affections, employed to designate friendship and love.

No one, save Montaigne, has better described than Aristotle the pleasures and the delights of friendship:

" For the presence itself of friends is delightful both in prosperity and adversity; since the grief of those who are in affliction is lightened when their friends participate of their sorrow. Hence, likewise, it may be doubted whether friends share a part of the affliction of their friends, as if it were part of a burden. Or is this not the case: that the presence of friends being delightful, the conception that they participate of the sorrow produces a diminution of the grief ? For a friend possesses a consoling power, both in his presence and his words, if he is dexterous, since he knows the manners of his friend, and with what he is pleased and pained." [1]

" But in the friendship I speak of," says Montaigne, "our souls mix and work themselves into one piece with so universal a mixture that there is no more sign of the seam by which they were first conjoined. Our souls are drawn so unanimously together, and we have with so mutual a confidence laid open the very bottom

[1] Aristotle, *Ethics*, book ix., ch. xi.

of our hearts to one another's view, that I not only know his as well as my own ; but should certainly, in any concern of mine, have trusted my interest much more willingly with him than with myself." [1]

267. The Ideal Inclinations. — It remains to say a few words of the third category of ou- inclinations, which we call *ideal* for lack of a better term. They are sometimes called "higher" inclinations ; but we refuse to admit that, in the way of inclination, there is anything higher than paternal love or patriotic feeling. The word ideal, on the contrary, is justified as a designation for these emotions of a wholly particular class, because ideas, as intellectual elements, play a preponderant part in them. These inclinations are neither more humane nor more disinterested than the social inclinations ; but their principal characteristic is that they are not connected with persons, but are derived from a pronounced development of the reason and of general ideas, and correspond to a certain degree of culture.

268. Division of the Ideal Inclinations. — It is not proposed to describe these inclinations in detail, but in a summary way to enumerate and characterize them.

Some are connected with the *true*, or with science. These are the scientific inclinations.

Others are connected with the *good*, or with virtue. These are the moral feelings.

Still others are connected with the *beautiful*, or the fine arts. These are the æsthetic* inclinations.

. [1] Montaigne, *Essays*, book i., ch. xxvii.

Finally, we must include in this category of ideal inclinations, the feeling to which the idea of God gives rise, — the religious feeling.

269. Love of the True. — If we recall what has been said of the origin of pleasure, — that it always has its origin in activity, — we shall comprehend without difficulty that thought, from the very fact that it acts and enters into possession of its object, which is truth, that thought in this commerce experiences veritable delights.

The great scholars who discover new truths experience more than other men the pleasures of thought. But no man is a stranger to them, and we all know the joys of reading, of study, and of scientific research.

Montesquieu * said, " I have never felt a chagrin for which an hour of reading has not consoled me."

" With study," said Augustin Thierry,* " we traverse evil days without feeling their weight ; we create our own destiny and employ our life nobly. This is what I have done, and what I would do again if I had to begin the journey of life over again. Blind and suffering, without hope and almost without respite, I can give myself this testimony, which on my part will never be suspected : there is something that is worth more than material joys, more than fortune, more than health itself, — this is devotion to science." [1]

270. Moral Sentiments. — We are sensible of the good as well as of the true. Virtue excites our admiration

[1] A. Thierry, *Dix ans d'études,* Preface.

in others, and our gratification in ourselves. We take delight in contemplating the noble actions of others; and we rejoice in whatever of good we have been able to do ourselves.

So, also, evil excites our aversion. We feel a repugnance, a horror, for the crimes committed by our fellows. We reprove ourselves for the evil we have done; we repent of it, we feel remorse for it.

These feelings, joined to the idea of the good and to the idea of duty, constitute what is called, by a single word, the moral consciousness, the exact description of which will find its natural place in our *Éléments de morale*.

271. Æsthetic Sentiments. — The very varied inclinations which we feel for the different manifestations of the beautiful, either in art or in nature, are called the æsthetic * sentiments.

The beautiful is much more difficult to define than the good and the true. The true is evidently the conformity of thought with reality; and the good, the conformity of action with the moral law. But what shall be said of the beautiful? In truth, no one of the formulas proposed by philosophers is satisfactory;[1] and we must perhaps be content to define the beautiful by the characteristic emotion which it excites in our hearts, — *admiration.*

---

[1] H. Marion defines the beautiful as "the intelligible, the perfect, the rational clothed in sensible forms." But what is there rational in beautiful colors? And what sensible forms are there in a noble act of patriotism, or of family devotion?

In default of a general definition of the beautiful, it is still possible to find particular definitions for the different species of beauty. Moral beauty is the perfection of virtue; physical beauty is regularity of features associated with a certain expression.

The beautiful is doubtless a conception of our reason; but the beautiful varies in nature with each of the arts, poetry, painting, music, etc., which seek to express it. Each artist has an ideal which he pursues, and this ideal is doubtless derived from the reason, in so far as it is the studied purpose, the innate tendency of nature; but it is the experience of each one, and the conditions peculiar to each art, which more or less determine and realize this ideal.

The beautiful ought, moreover, to be distinguished from the pretty and the sublime. The pretty is not merely a diminutive of the beautiful; it is something particular and indefinable which is connected with proportions less grand. The sublime, on the contrary, supposes colossal proportions and always implies something extraordinary and even inordinate.

The æsthetic feelings are the source of very keen enjoyments, but they require a special culture and a true intellectual refinement.

But the beautiful does not exist merely in art and in the creations of man; we also look for it and love it in nature.

272. The Feeling of Nature. — The feeling of nature

forms a part of that category of complex feelings which are not developed in all men, which are not contemporary with all the ages of humanity.

Milton,* in his "Paradise Lost," ascribes this language to Eve : —

> " Sweet is the breath of morn, her rising sweet,
> With charm of earliest birds; pleasant the sun,
> When first on this delightful land he spreads
> His orient beams, and sweet the coming on
> Of grateful ev'ning mild; then silent night
> With this her solemn bird and this fair moon,
> And these the gems of heaven, her starry train."

The first of the race had not the leisure to devote themselves to these poetic contemplations, and nature, with all the obstacles which she opposed to the peace of their existence, could scarcely provoke their admiration.

The feeling of nature is a complex feeling, which supposes a great number of elements, and which can be developed in the human heart only when humanity has risen to a certain degree of intellectual culture. Nature speaks at once to our senses, to our scientific intelligence, and to our religious instincts. The love of nature evidently contains sense-elements, as the attractions of brilliant colors and harmonious lines ; but it is modified in a thousand ways by the scientific or religious ideas which are mingled with it. "The atheists," said Rousseau, "do not love the country."

At all events they love it differently from religious
men, who, back of nature, see the creative action of
God.

273. The Religious Sentiment.—The religious sentiment, like the other ideal feelings, is intimately connected with intellectual facts. It evidently exists only
in souls where religious beliefs have been developed.
Wherever the idea of God is absent, the religious sentiment disappears with it. It varies, however, with the
forms, so diverse, which religion assumes. With primitive peoples, it was a feeling of fear and terror with
respect to the malevolent and terrible divinities. Then
man recognized, little by little, the divine goodness, or
at least the beneficent influence of the forces of nature.
Since then, the religious sentiment, without ceasing to
be a fear, has consisted chiefly of love and gratitude, of
confidence and repose.

It is particularly with respect to the intellectual and
ideal feelings, that the sensibility varies with the times
and with the progress of the centuries. We love different things from what our ancestors loved, and we
love the same things differently. Though psychology
may do its best, it cannot grasp in all their shades,
those delicate feelings which are incessantly modifying
themselves, and which take almost as many forms as
there are individuals. There are a hundred ways of
loving the beautiful; and there are also a hundred ways
of loving God.

SUMMARY.

156. The common characteristic of the **SOCIAL INCLI-NATIONS** is that they are **DISINTERESTED**; they alone make us truly capable of loving.

157. The social inclinations comprise : — (1) the love of other men in general, or **SOCIABILITY**; (2) the love of our parents, or the **FAMILY AFFECTIONS**; (3) the love of our fellow-citizens, or the **PATRIOTIC AFFECTIONS**; (4) the elective or individual affections, as **FRIENDSHIP** and **LOVE**.

158. SOCIABILITY is a natural fact ; habit sometimes makes us insensible to the pleasures derived from it ; but in isolation we keenly feel the need of the company of our fellows.

159. Sociability and the other affectionate inclinations have their common source in **SYMPATHY**.

160. Sympathy is at once the tendency to bring our feelings into accord with the feelings of our fellows, and to love those who have the same feelings, the same nature, that we have.

161. Moralists who, like **LA ROCHEFOUCAULD**, pretend to reduce all our feelings to self-love, calumniate human nature. The pleasure which accompanies the affections is not their cause and the reason of their existence ; it is but their consequence, and accompanies only the affections which are sincere and true.

162. The family affections, and the patriotic affections, are **NATURAL**, and do not depend upon choice. Friendship and love, on the contrary, suppose a deliberate preference, and this is why they are called **ELECTIVE AFFECTIONS**.

163. The ideal inclinations all suppose a certain intellectual culture; they are connected with the **IDEA OF THE TRUE**, with the **IDEA OF THE GOOD**, with the **IDEA OF THE BEAUTIFUL**, and with the **IDEA OF GOD**.

CHAPTER XVI

THE WILL AND HABIT

274. Voluntary Activity. — The activity recognized as the basis of the actions which manifest themselves, or may manifest themselves, through external movements, presents, as we know, three forms : instinct, will, and habit.

We have studied instinctive activity (see Chapter II.); and we are now to examine voluntary activity and the activity of habit.

275. Definition of the Will. — The proper domain of the will, as of the two other forms of activity, is, as we have just remarked, actions properly so called ; that is, inward acts followed by effects or external movements.

The will may be defined : *The power which the mind has of determining itself, with consciousness and reflection, spontaneously and freely, to an action of its choice.*

276. Will in the Child. — Will, thus understood, is, like the conscious reason, the prerogative of man. Doubtless the child acts and resolves ; but instinct and sensibility, and not will, are the principles of his determinations and acts. The child is a voluntary agent, but he does not have will.

277. Essential Characteristics of the Will. — The essen-

tial characteristics of the will are reflection and, consequently, liberty. (See Chapter XVII.) Voluntary acts
are reflective and, consequently, free; that is, they depend only upon ourselves.

278. Relations of the Will to Other Faculties. — The
will is sharply distinguished from the intelligence and
the sensibility. It is not within our power to experience, or not to experience, a given feeling, or to have
one thought rather than another; but, as we understand the term, we are masters of our will.[1]

To the philosophers who confound will with desire,
that is, with sensibility, it must be said in reply that, in
fact, when desire and will are in accord and co-exist, we
do not confound the attraction exercised by the thing
desired with the power which we have of yielding to
that attraction; that, in the second place, it often
happens to us to desire without willing; and, finally,
that desire and will are in certain cases contradictory;
then there is a struggle, a conflict, and at one time it
is the desire, and at another the will, which carries the
day.

To those who confound the will with the intelligence,
it is to be said, in reply, that if all will is grafted on an
idea, it is nevertheless not the same thing as the idea.
How many ideas present themselves to our mind which
are not followed by volition! Socrates surely deceived

---

[1] In our *Lectures on Pedagogy* (Chapter XI.), we have discussed at length the
differences which distinguish the will from the intelligence and the sensibility.

himself when he confounded "knowledge" with "virtue." It is one thing to think the good, but another thing to will it. It is, nevertheless, true that the will, though something distinct and irreducible, has intimate relations with the sensibility and with the intelligence. An analysis of the different elements of a voluntary act will bring these relations clearly to light.

279. Analysis of a Voluntary Act. — Every voluntary action, when complete, supposes several elements :

1. THE CONCEPTION, or the idea of the act to be accomplished.

2. DELIBERATION, that is, an examination of the motives or of the mobiles which influence us to act in one way or in another.

3. DETERMINATION, or resolution, which is the proper act of the will, — the firm decision which we make to determine ourselves to a given act.

4. THE EXECUTION, which follows the resolution.

280. Conception of the Act to be accomplished. — It is useless to insist on this first condition of the voluntary act. It is evident that we act voluntarily only when, the intelligence preceding the will, we have an idea of the action to be accomplished and also an idea of a contrary action.

Before saying "I will go out," I represent to myself, intellectually, either the walk, or the fact of remaining at home.

281. Deliberation. — The intelligence does not present

to us merely the idea of the act to which we are presently to determine ourselves, but it also suggests to us
the reasons or motives for which we ought to prefer
this act to every other. It is pleasant, or we have the
leisure, or we need to take exercise, etc. ; but all these
reasons for going out may be counterbalanced by contrary or opposite reasons ; we are expecting a visit, or
we do not know in what direction to go, etc.

282. Motives and Mobiles. — But the intelligence does
not intervene alone in deliberation. The sensibility,
with its desires and inclinations, enters also into line,
and throws into the scale the weight of its peculiar
influence. By going out we are assured of meeting a
friend whom we desire to see ; or, our walk will lead us
to a museum where we anticipate the artistic pleasures
of which we are fond.

In other words, deliberation bears at the same time
on reasons of the intellectual order, which are called
motives, and on reasons of the sensitive order, which
are called the *mobiles* of our actions.

283. Every Voluntary Action is Deliberate. — Sometimes the deliberation is very long because the decision to
be taken is of some importance, or because the individual who deliberates is of a hesitating disposition.

Victor Hugo, in the chapter of his *Misérables* entitled " Une Tempête sous une crâne," has admirably
described that long train of thoughts and feelings which
a man may traverse before determining himself to act.

Sometimes, also, the deliberation is very short, — we are in a hurry to act, and must come to a decision at once. Volition, in this case, is almost instantaneous, but it always supposes that by a rapid glance we have compared and weighed the pros and the cons.

284. Determination. — It is in determination or decision that the will essentially resides. Up to a certain moment we oscillate, so to speak, between two contrary resolutions ; we load in succession the two sides of the balance which by turns rise or fall. But there comes a moment which is the crisis of the will, so to speak, when we no longer hesitate, when we turn resolutely to one side and finally determine our conduct.

Whatever attraction our desires exercise over us, whatever influence we grant to our thoughts, it is neither our desires nor our thoughts which determine us, but we ourselves come to a resolution, sometimes by the aid of our desires, and sometimes in opposition to them, by certain motives which we place above contrary motives.

285. Execution. — It has just been said that a voluntary act consists especially in determination, whether it be followed by an effect or not. In general, however, execution accompanies volition ; and in order that the voluntary act may be really complete, it is not only necessary that it should be resolved on, but that an effort should be made to execute it.

The execution itself depends on external circumstances independent of my will. My paralyzed hand may refuse to obey when I command it to write ; my muscles may be too weak to comply with the resolution which I have taken to raise a weight which is too heavy. But even in cases where the orders of my will have not been executed, an order has been given, and there have been an effort and a commencement of execution.

Will, not followed by an effect, remains incomplete ; it is as yet but an *intention*.

286. Importance of the Will. — It is the will which makes the human personality, which really creates the Ego ; it is through the will that we are finally ourselves.

"Our authority over ourselves," says Jouffroy,* "is maintained only by continual exercise. . . . The measure of this authority is also that of the human dignity, because this authority is the man himself." [1]

287. Character. — The best man is he who has mind, heart, and character. Now it is especially on the will that depends this third quality of an accomplished man. Character, in fact, supposes a firm will which can resist the caprices and the fluctuations of the sensibility ; which governs itself and pursues its aim with an inflexible tenacity, without allowing itself to be turned aside either by the suggestions of other men, or by the solicitations of the passions.

[1] Ch. Jouffroy, *Mélanges philosophiques*, p. 361.

288. Habit. — Voluntary activity is not the most ordinary form of human activity. Issuing from instinct, activity rises to the voluntary mode only to fall back into habit and to repose there. The greater number of our actions are derived from habit. We write, we speak, we walk, we accomplish most of the actions of our life, not with reflection and by a ceaselessly renewed effort of our will, but under the mild and feeble influence of custom.

289. Characteristics of Habit. — Habit is then an irreflective, mechanical, and automatic mode of activity. It has all the characteristics of instinct, — sureness and infallibility ; but it differs from it in its origin. Instinct, so to speak, is really an hereditary habit which is transmitted to us through our ancestors and which manifests itself immediately in the living being. Habit, on the contrary, is acquired ; it results from our former acts and supposes a previous will ; it is a second nature.

290. Origin of Habit. — Habit is derived from a repetition of the same act, or from a continuation of the same impression. Habit, in fact, extends its empire not only over our voluntary actions, which by repeating themselves gradually lose their characteristic of reflective actions, or actions accomplished with effort ; but also over our sensations, our intellectual operations, our feelings, — in a word, over all our states of consciousness. Consequently, habit is the result either of a voluntary action accomplished by the individual, or an action exerted on that individual by external agents, such, for example, as temperature, heat and cold, light, etc.

The more the action has been repeated, and the more the impression has been prolonged, the more the habit will tend to develop itself and the more force it will acquire. But it has justly been remarked that the repetition of an action, or the continuation of an impression, is not necessary to explain the beginning of habit. In truth, one single act, or one single impression, suffices in order that habit may have a tendency to appear.

291. Effects of Habit. — Habit exercises different effects on the human faculties. On the one hand, it facilitates action, supplies the place of the will, sharpens the intelligence, and strengthens the inclinations ; on the other hand, it blunts the sensations.

292. It facilitates Action. — Under the empire of habit, we come to repeat without effort acts which, at first, had been painful and laborious.

"Through habit we daily accomplish wonders. . . . Enter a printing office. All the workmen are very far from having the same merit ; but the least intelligent and the least capable will select from the case letters which they need, and arrange them in place with a promptness and sureness of touch which resemble instinct. It *is* instinct, in fact, for it is habit." [1]

[1] J. Simon, *Devoir*, p. 364.

293. It supplies the Place of the Will. — Our life would be singularly retarded, and our actions would be reduced to a small compass, if we were obliged to reflect and to will every time we act.

" This act of walking, which seems to us so simple, would be for man a subject of preoccupation and study all his life. We would speak our native tongue with the same effort which the use of a foreign language, newly and imperfectly learned, would require. The search for words and the preoccupation with the syntax would prevent our mind from devoting itself wholly to the pursuit of the thought. In writing, we would resemble a scholar who painfully follows a copy ; it would be necessary to devote ourselves to painting each letter. The man the most gifted would not succeed in playing five measures on the piano without stopping to take breath."

294. It tends to renew Action. — By the effect of habit we not only acquire greater facility in executing the acts which it directs, but we are disposed to reproduce them oftener. The force of habit determines a tendency or inclination to recommence what has once been done.

295. It sharpens the Intelligence. — Through habit, we become more skilled in discerning the elements of perceptions and in analyzing the sources of our ideas. Our intellectual powers are strengthened under its influence.

"Musicians are able to decompose an orchestra, and to distinguish in the general effect the part of each instrument.

"The leader of an orchestra hears all the musicians at once, and he hears each of them. . . . It is to active habit, that is, to practice frequently repeated, that the violin-player owes the facility with which he can at the same moment read the notes, run over the finger-board of his instrument, manipulate the bow, and remain sufficiently master of himself to appreciate the effect which he produces on his hearers, and to enjoy, as they do, and even more than they do, the charm of the music.

"Who reasons well? Is it he who knows by heart all the rules of Aristotle, or he who, by daily practice, has accustomed himself to argumentation?"[1]

296. It enfeebles the Consciousness. — But it is the nature of habit to produce contradictory effects. If, on the one hand, it fortifies the active faculties of perception, judgment, and reasoning, and the intellectual faculties in general, it must be recollected, on the other hand, that it enfeebles, and may gradually suppress, the consciousness.

A phenomenon which is repeated and which is habitual to us becomes insensible. We do not feel the weight of the air which rests upon us. The chemist lives among foul odors without smelling them.

---

[1] J. Simon, *op. cit.*

An act which is often renewed becomes unconscious. In writing, we have scarcely any consciousness of the letters which we form. In playing a piece upon the piano, we no longer take account of the movements which we execute.

297. Effects of Habit on the Sensibility. — In its action on the sensibility, the influence of habit is also double and contradictory :

1. It blunts the sensations of pleasure and pain.

2. It increases the strength of the inclinations.

One of the best-known effects of habit is that it dulls our joys and sorrows. We accustom ourselves to evils that at first we most detested ; and we become insensible to the pleasures that were at first the keenest. On the other hand, the affectionate feelings, the inclinations, and the passions, at least in their beginning, and up to a certain limit beyond which satiety begins, augment in power under the influence of habit. " Will one love society," says Janet, "if he does not often go there? travel, if he has never travelled? or reading, if he has not read ?"

298. The Laws of Habit. — It is thus that habit at one time blunts, and at another sharpens, and by turns enfeebles or strengthens, our faculties of every class. An attempt has been made to reduce these contrary effects to one general law, as follows : " Habit enfeebles all *passive* impressions, and develops all the *active* operations."

"The change in a living being which comes to him from without, becomes to him more and more foreign; the change which has come to him from himself, becomes more and more his own. *Receptivity* diminishes, and *spontaneity* * increases; . . . continuity or repetition enfeebles *passivity,** but exalts *activity.*" [1]

Thus are reconciled the apparently contradictory results of habit, which in fact can augment and strengthen the active powers of the soul, only because it diminishes by the same act the vivacity of our impressions and of whatever there is of the purely passive in our acts.

299. Importance of Habit. — It is not exaggeration to attribute to habit a preponderant part in human life. It is habit which consolidates the results of our efforts, and spares us from making a constant appeal to the costly and laborious exercise of our will. Without it, everything must be recommenced over and over again; by means of it, we profit by all that we have done. Through habit we doubtless tend to become automata,* but intelligent automata who do over again without trouble only what we have once willed to do. It is habit, as Albert Lemoine * has justly said, "which fixes the perpetual *becoming* of our existence, which arrests time that nothing arrests. . . . By means of habit, the past in the living being is not abolished. . . . By it, the past accumulates and is included in the present. It holds this past, and still retains it in its possession under this

[1] M. Ravaisson, *De l'Habitude*, p. 9.

concise form; it has augmented its substance, and has assimilated it to its own nature."

But habit naturally keeps alive the evil as well as the good. It is habit which makes the unity of our life and adds the present minute to all those which have preceded. According to the use which we have made of our activity in the past, shall we be determined in the present and in the future to actions which are good or bad. Habit is a servitude, since it makes us the slaves of our past; but it has depended upon ourselves whether this past shall lead us on to virtue, to knowledge, and to truth.

SUMMARY.

164. Human activity manifests itself under three forms: **INSTINCT, WILL,** and **HABIT**.

165. VOLUNTARY ACTIVITY, or **WILL**, is the power which we have of **SELF-DETERMINATION WITH RE-FLECTION** and through a **FREE CHOICE**.

166. The will must be confounded neither with **DESIRE** nor with **IDEA**.

167. A complete voluntary act comprises four elements: the **CONCEPTION** of the act to be accomplished, **DELIB-ERATION, DETERMINATION,** and **EXECUTION**.

168. DELIBERATION brings motives and mobiles face to face, that is, the intellectual reasons and the solicitations of the sensibility.

169. DETERMINATION or decision is the characteristic act of the will.

170. EXECUTION, or at least a beginning of execution, an effort to accomplish the act to which one has determined himself, is the necessary complement of the voluntary act.

171. The will truly creates the **HUMAN PERSON- ALITY**. Our dignity is measured by the authority which we have acquired over ourselves.

172. HABIT is the **IRREFLECTIVE AUTOMATIC ACTIVITY** which succeeds voluntary activity.

173. Habit has all the characteristics of **INSTINCT**, but it differs from it in origin ; it is an acquired instinct, a second nature.

174. The power of habit depends on the frequency of the repetitions of the same act, or on a prolongation of the same impression.

175. The effect of habit is to **FACILITATE ACTION** and to dispose us to renew it.

176. It fortifies the active faculties of the intelligence, but it **ENFEEBLES THE CONSCIOUSNESS**.

177. It enfeebles the sensations of pleasure and pain, but it stimulates the inclinations.

178. In a word, habit **ENFEEBLES** all the **PASSIVE IMPRESSIONS**, but **DEVELOPS** all the **ACTIVE OPER- ATIONS**.

CHAPTER XVII

LIBERTY AND DETERMINISM

300. Different Senses of the Word Liberty. — Leibnitz was right in saying that "the term *liberty* is very ambiguous." There is no term more widely employed, and none more poorly defined.

The term liberty is first applied to physical actions, or material movements which do not encounter obstacles, but which are accomplished without hindrance. The water runs freely, the animal moves about freely. This is *physical liberty*, which is equivalent simply to the absence of obstacles.

Civil liberty and *political liberty* have also a significa-tion wholly their own. Civil liberty is the consecration, through law, of the natural rights of man, — property, inviolability of person and domicile, etc. Political liberty is the complement of rights through which the citizen co-operates in the government of his country, — liberty of the press, liberty of assemblage, universal suffrage, etc.

Finally, we call *moral liberty* or *free-will,** the power attributed to man of self-determination according to his will, of deciding on one course of action rather than another, according to his choice; in a word, as Condillac said, "of doing what he does not do, and of not doing what he does do."

301. Free-Will. — It is solely with this last form of liberty that we have to concern ourselves. The question to resolve is, whether man, when he acts voluntarily, is really capable of resisting the impulses of his sensibility and of choosing between the different motives which his intelligence suggests to him ; or whether, on the contrary, his resolutions are the enforced consequences either of an external necessity, or of fatalities of temperament, or, finally, of a psychological determinism.

302. The Liberty of Indifference. — It is first necessary to exclude, in order to state the object of discussion with precision, certain false interpretations of liberty. According to certain philosophers of the Middle Age, man has the power to determine his conduct without motive ; this is what is called the *liberty of indifference*. A classical example is that of Buridan's ass, which this philosopher imagined placed at an equal distance from two bundles of hay of equal size, and equally inviting. The animal, divided between these two equal temptations, would have, by virtue of the liberty of indifference, the power to direct himself at his choice towards one or towards the other. Bossuet and Reid have revived the same thesis. Liberty, according to them, is determined arbitrarily without motive. "Why," says Reid, "when you are presented with several coins of the same value, do you take one rather than another ?" It is in this circumstance, that is, in an act absolutely indeterminate, that liberty consists.

It is too easy to reply that the liberty of indifference is a pure assumption ; that in our important acts there is always a motive according to which we determine our conduct ; finally, that the insignificant acts in which motive does not appear are in no respects free acts, but are acts of caprice or hazard in which free-will has no part.

In fact, voluntary acts always suppose the presence of a motive, and we have seen (Chapter XVII.), that the resolutions or determinations of the will are always reflective, and that they are based on intellectual reasons.

If liberty exists, it is then within the limits created by the presence of one or more motives. The liberty of indifference would be a pure miracle, which it is impossible to conceive. We cannot imagine, in fact, a liberty which would determine itself in a void, without reason, by a sort of *coup d'état* of the will. Either liberty does not exist, or else it is and can be but the choice between motives which influence us in contrary directions.

303. Objection drawn from Motives. — It is precisely from the necessary presence of motives in every free determination, that the philosophers who deny free-will have drawn their most formidable argument. Of several motives presented, it is said, it is the strongest which will always prevail. The soul is like a balance whose pans are loaded ; the beam always inclines in the direction of the pan which supports the heavier weight. There can, therefore, be no such thing as liberty, for the mind is determined by the strongest motive.

304. Refutation of this Objection. — The objection would be irrefutable if we knew in advance what motive is the strongest. The weights of the balance have a determined value, say of fifty or a hundred pounds ; and in whatever way they are placed in the pan, they there preserve an influence equal to their weight. On the contrary, the motives which present themselves to our mind, and which intervene in the deliberations of our will, have no absolute value. Who has not many times learned by experience that we sometimes prefer an insignificant motive to an important motive ? The strength of the motive is derived, in part at least, from what our will adds of itself to its natural power. The reasons for acting are not decisive by themselves ; they become so only through the consent of the will. The proof is that we cannot know in advance and predict what will be, in the will of another man or in our own will, the strongest motive. The strongest motive is that according to which we determine our conduct, but we do not know that it is the strongest until after our will has declared itself. The objection drawn from motives, then, leaves the question open, and it is nowise proved that motive is the determining cause of our action.

305. Proofs of Liberty. — Are the proofs of liberty of a nature to confirm and warrant the common belief? This is what we now have to examine.

These proofs are : (1) The consciousness which we have of it, the direct or psychological proof. (2) The moral proofs, — the moral concept and the responsibility of duty suppose liberty ; — these are the indirect proofs based on reasoning and on the consequences involved in the denial of liberty.

306. Consciousness of Liberty. — All the philosophers who believe in liberty have appealed to consciousness.

" Liberty," said Bossuet, " is proved by the evidence of feeling and experience. Let each one of us listen to himself and consult himself, and he will feel that he is free, just as he will feel that he is reasonable."

In fact, if we will consult ourselves, it seems that liberty is not a doubtful question. When we deliberate on a decision to be taken, we are conscious of the power to act in one way or in another. Deliberation would be a snare and a deceit if we were not free to decide as we please.

And so in the decision itself, the feeling of liberty is present to our consciousness ; we believe that it depends upon ourselves to suspend our resolution or to persevere in it. The act once accomplished, the same consciousness persists : we repent of having done what we have, or we congratulate ourselves on it ; which proves that we are conscious of having been able to act differently. In a word, the possibility of doing what we have not done, or of not doing what we have done, is an element inherent in the consciousness of all our voluntary acts.

307. Objections of Bayle and Spinoza. — But this consciousness of liberty has been considered as an illusion by a great number of philosophers, notably by Bayle * and Spinoza.*

" If the magnetic needle," says Bayle, "which the magnetic force turns toward the north, or the weather-cock which the wind drives, were conscious of their movements without knowing their cause, they would ascribe the honor of them to themselves and would attribute to themselves their intention."

Hobbes had already said to the same effect : If the top which children spin were conscious of its motion, it would think that this motion proceeded from its own will, unless it feels who whips it. Thus man does in his actions, because he does not know what the whips are which determine his will.

And Spinoza held, in turn, that "the pretended consciousness of liberty is but ignorance of the causes which make us act."

The comparisons of Hobbes and Bayle are wholly inexact, and the explanation of Spinoza is in contradiction with experience.

In fact, we cannot confound the desire which these philosophers attribute to the top and the weathercock, with the will, nor the execution of the action with the decision which precedes it.

Now, in the examples cited, there is the hypothesis of a desire felt by the weathercock, and the hypothesis of a movement executed by the top; but there is not the reflective and deliberate determination which is the characteristic of a voluntary action as we experience it in ourselves.

Moreover, it is so far from being true that the consciousness of liberty is ignorance of the motives which make us act, that, on the contrary, this consciousness is as much the more vivid as we the better understand the motives according to which we determine our conduct. It is only in circumstances where we act with reflection, in full consciousness of cause, that we believe that we act freely. On the contrary, every time we accomplish acts of which we do not render to ourselves an account, and are determined by concealed or unknown reasons, or by blind impulses, we have no thought of attributing these actions to our liberty. It would be, then, more just to say that the consciousness of liberty coincides with the knowledge of the motives by which we determine our conduct. The feeling of liberty is perhaps an illusion, but surely this illusion does not depend on an ignorance of the motives which preside over our determination.

308. Moral Proofs. — The moral proofs of liberty are indirect proofs which consist in saying, in a general way : If liberty does not exist, the moral concepts of obligation, duty, and responsibility must disappear; they have no longer a meaning, and every reason for their existence is lacking.

Duty really implies power. The moral law orders me to do what is good, but its orders are a mockery if I have not the power to obey them.

Without liberty, responsibility is a chimera. I feel myself responsible for whatever I do freely, for my faults and my vices ; I accept no responsibility for my natural infirmities if I am deformed, nor for my diseases if they come from nature and not from my acts.

It is evident that morals and the existence of liberty are mutually dependent. If you deny liberty, there are merely creatures beautiful, ugly, useful, or dangerous ; but there are no longer good or bad, virtuous or vicious, men.

"No one reprehends those who are naturally deformed," said Aristotle ; " but we blame those who are so through the want of exercise, and from negligence. The like also takes place in imbecility and mutilation. For no one would reproach a man who is blind from nature, or disease, or a blow, but would rather pity him ; but every one would reprove him who is blind for drinking wine to excess, or for any other species of intemperance." [1]

1 Aristotle, *Ethics*, chapter v., p. 93.

309. Universal Belief in Liberty. — All the facts of human life give evidence of a universal belief in liberty. Without it, it is impossible to explain promises, contracts, punishments and rewards, exhortations and threats, repentance, etc.

If I am not free, a promise becomes nonsense. In fact, I shall either be fatally doomed to do what I promise, and then why bind myself by a useless promise? or else I shall be fatally constrained to do the contrary, and then the engagement which I make is absurd.

So also punishments and rewards are legitimate only when they are addressed to free agents, really responsible for their actions.

"Is not man," says Aristotle, "the father of his actions as he is of his children? This question is answered in the affirmative by the conduct of all men and by the testimony of legislators. They punish and chastise those who commit culpable acts, whenever these acts are not the result of constraint or ignorance for which the agent is not responsible. On the contrary, they honor and reward the authors of virtuous actions; but in all the actions which do not depend on ourselves, no one thinks of forcing us to do them. For example, every one knows that it would be useless to exhort us not to feel warm, or not to suffer from cold or hunger, or not to experience certain sensations, for our sufferings would be none the less on account of these exhortations." In fact, it would be useless to resort to exhortation or to threats, if the agent to whom we address ourselves is not free to modify his resolutions and acts in the direction which we point out to him.

The whole of human life, in its institutions and laws, is founded on the belief in liberty.

" I do not perform an act, I do not pronounce a word, which does not suppose a belief in my liberty and in that of others. What is the law which men discuss and promulgate with formal preparation? What is the tribunal where they call on God to witness their judgments? What is the scaffold where they take the honor and life of their brother in expiation of a crime? Deny the belief in liberty, and society falls to pieces." [1]

But it will be said that all this simply proves that men believe in liberty, but not that they are right in believing in it. We reply, that a fact so universal has many chances of being in conformity with reality; and that, after all, it is sufficient for us to believe naturally in liberty and to be invincibly led to believe in it, even if the arguments of philosophers were to succeed in inspiring us with some doubts in the solidity of our belief.

310. Different Forms of Fatalism. — At all times liberty has been called in question and denied : but fatalism, or the denial of liberty, has taken, either in religious beliefs or in philosophical systems, a great number of forms.

311. Theological Fatalism. — Among the ancients and

[1] J. Simon, *Le Devoir.*

among the Mohammedans, in the pantheistic philosophy, a place is made above humanity for a superior
force or divinity whose will governs all events and
forbids to man all liberty. This mysterious power is
what the Greeks and the Romans called destiny, *fatum.*
Whatever efforts man may make to struggle against
destiny, he goes where destiny leads him. The Mussul-
mans say, "It was written."

Even in the Christian religion, there remain some
traces of this conception of destiny, presented, it is
true, under the feature of a personal God, the absolute
master of all the events of this world. "Man is rest-
less, and God directs him."

The idea of *grace* * the first condition of virtue, that
is, of a mysterious inspiration of God predisposing his
privileged creatures to the good, has direct relations
with fatalism. In some Christian sects, belief in predestination * has become a dogma.

These are the old forms of fatalism, and modern
science does not need to occupy itself with them.

312. Physiological Fatalism. — Other fatalists have
invoked, as determining causes of human actions, cli-
màte, race, temperament, and, finally, the physiological
conditions of man's moral faculties.

"Without a material modification in the nervous
system, and also in the brain," says Moleschott,* "voluntary movements do not take place.

"But this modification comes from without. The

modification stands to the excitation, as an effect to the cause which produces it.

"This reason makes it appear, in a manner wholly convincing, that the movement does not emanate from a so-called free will.

" It will be better to say, that the will is the necessary expression of a state of the brain produced by external influences.

" Man is the resultant of his ancestors, of his nurse, of the place and the moment, of the air and the weather, of the sound and the light, of his diet and his clothing. His will is the consequence of all these causes ; it is tied to a law of nature which we recognize in its manifestation, as a planet to its orbit, or a plant to the soil on which it grows." [1]

These are exaggerations which nothing can justify. Surely temperament, physiological conditions, and external influences, limit the human will and contract the circle in which it moves, but all these causes, whatever may be their power, by no means suppress liberty. Man is dependent on nature ; but he finds in himself a point of support for resisting external influences and for maintaining his personal independence.

313. Psychological Fatalism or Determinism. — The truly modern and scientific form of fatalism is psychological determinism.

We have already stated what reply can be made to its

1 Moleschott, *La Circulation de la Vie*, t. ii., p. 149.

mode of reasoning, founded exclusively on the necessary relation of cause to effect, and on the absolutely
decisive influence which motives, that is, causes, exercise on the actions which are their effects.

Doubtless something must be granted to the determinists; we must recognize with them that at a given
moment of our existence our liberty is not entire and
absolute. We have not the power to break brusquely
with our past, and to absolve ourselves from all solidar-
ity with what we have previously done. No, we must
count with the influence of our habits and our inveter-
ate tendencies; but even under these conditions there
remains a part for our will to play.

The determinists say that liberty is a solution of
continuity in the necessary concatenation of effects
and causes. They would be right, if we were speaking
of a liberty absolutely independent, indeterminate, and
absolved from every condition. But the will is precisely the cause which is at work in our free resolutions;
and this efficient cause* determines itself in view of
another cause which is the end to be attained, or the
purpose pursued with reflection; in a word, the final
cause of our action.

314. Liberty and Reason. — Liberty is, then, nothing
other than the power of acting in accordance with ideas,
or, in other terms, the power of obeying the reason. The
more reasonable we are, the freer we are. We are then
free, in the sense of becoming more free, of incessantly

enlarging our liberty. It depends upon our efforts to absolve ourselves more and more from the impulses of instinct, the solicitations of the sensibility, the caprices of irreflection, and to be more capable of possessing and governing ourselves, by augmenting the part of reflection and reason in our conduct.

SUMMARY.

179. MORAL LIBERTY is to be confounded neither with physical liberty, civil liberty, nor political liberty.

180. Moral liberty, or **FREE-WILL**, is the power of determining ourselves voluntarily to an action which we choose.

181. It is not exact to say that liberty determines itself arbitrarily, as the partisans of the **LIBERTY OF INDIF-FERENCE** understand it.

182. Liberty determines itself **ACCORDING TO A MOTIVE**; but this motive becomes the strongest only because the will **CHOOSES** it.

183. The proofs of liberty are the **DIRECT CON-SCIOUSNESS** which we have of it, and the consequences which the denial of liberty involves, especially **IN MORALS**.

184. We are conscious of being free at the moment when we deliberate, when we decide on a course of conduct, and when we execute a voluntary action. This feeling of our liberty persists even after the action has been accomplished.

185. The consciousness of liberty is so far from being ignorance of the motives which cause us to act, that it is, on the contrary, the more vivid and the stronger as we have a better knowledge of the reasons according to which we determine our conduct.

186. The moral notions of **OBLIGATION, DUTY, RE-SPONSIBILITY, MERIT** and **DEMERIT,** are necessarily connected with the hypothesis of liberty. On the supposition that liberty does not exist, every system of morality falls to pieces.

187. Most of the facts of human life, the promises, exhortations, threats, rewards and punishments, etc., give proof of the **UNIVERSAL BELIEF** in liberty.

188. Fatalism, or the denial of liberty, has taken different forms ; sometimes it is theological, sometimes physiological, and sometimes psychological. Psychological **FATALISM** is called **DETERMINISM.**

189. Whatever influence we ascribe to the motives and the mobiles between which our will chooses and decides, there remains a field of action, limited, it is true, for liberty.

190. Through effort and the development of **REFLEC-TION** and **REASON**, we may enlarge our liberty.

CHAPTER XVIII

CONCLUSION OF THE PSYCHOLOGY. MIND AND BODY.

315. Rational Psychology. — The question of the existence of the soul. that is, of an immaterial principle, distinct and independent of the body, does not come within the domain of empirical psychology ; it belongs to rational psychology, or, in a word, to metaphysics.* Empirical psychology grasps only successive facts ; being an instrument of observation, it can merely describe, enumerate, and classify phenomena ; it cannot directly attain to the existence of what Kant called a *noumen,** that is, a principle superior and inaccessible to experience, a soul-substance, and the cause of thought. Without .wishing to go beyond the limits of this course, it is, nevertheless, necessary that we state, in concluding, the question of spiritualism and materialism, that is, of the two great doctrines which give two contrary solutions to the problem of the nature of the thinking principle, some separating it from the body, and others confounding it with the body.

316. Spiritualism and Materialism. — At all times, in fact, two contrary hypotheses have been face to face in the schools of philosophy. The first claims the great names of Plato, Aristotle, Descartes, Leibnitz, Kant, etc. ; it invokes the testimony of religion ; it is particularly a popular belief, a belief of common sense.

The second is authorized by a few philosophers, as Epicurus,* Holbach,* and Helvetius * ; by the philosophers of the eighteenth century in general ; and especially by modern physiologists whom the exclusive study of the brain has often led to deny the existence of the soul.

317. Duality of Human Nature. — It is undeniable that a natural instinct leads us to admit the duality of our being. In all times men have believed spontaneously in the distinction between the physical and the moral. On the one hand, they feel themselves riveted to matter ; and on the other, they aspire to the infinite, to the ideal, to the immaterial world. This Racine expressed in these verses imitated from the Holy Scriptures : —

" My God, what a cruel war ! Within me I find two men. . . . The one, all spirit and wholly divine, wills that, ceaselessly drawn toward heaven and encompassed by eternal blessings, I count all else as nothing ; while the other, by its baleful weight, holds me bent towards the earth." [1]

" What is the soul ? " asked a child of his mother. And, giving the reply himself, he added : " I have found it. It is with the soul that I love you."

From this duality of our being, from these contrary

---

[1] Racine, *Cantiques spirituels,* cantique iii.

and even contradictory tendencies, man has naturally been led to infer the co-existence in himself of two principles, mind and body.

318. Testimony of Consciousness. — To justify this distinction, reflective thought has believed that it finds a solid support in consciousness. The consciousness, according to Descartes and the philosophers of his school, directly reveals the existence of the soul. ·

" From the very fact that I know with certainty that I exist, and that, nevertheless, I do not observe that anything else necessarily belongs to my nature or to my essence, except that I am a thing which thinks, I conclude very correctly that my essence consists in this alone, — that I am a thing which thinks, or a substance whose whole essence or nature is but thought.

"And though perhaps, or rather certainly, as I just now said, I have a body to which I am strongly tied ; nevertheless, seeing that on the one hand I have a clear and distinct idea of myself, so far as I am merely a thing which thinks and is unextended, and that, on the other, I have a distinct idea of body so far as it is merely a thing extended which does not think ; it is certain that I, that is, my soul, through which I am what I am, is entirely and truly distinct from my body, and that it may be and may exist without me." [1]

For Descartes, then, the soul was more intelligible and easier to know than the body.

---

[1] Descartes, *Sixième Méditation.*

But it is very easy to reply to him that the body, whose non-existence he admits by hypothesis, nevertheless does not cease to exist because it is expedient for him to suppose that it does not exist. The distinction in consciousness between the two ideas, that of the body and that of the soul, is not equivalent to the real separation of the two existences. It is useless for Descartes to say that the essence of his being is simply to think ; this, on his part, is a pure assumption which does not suppress the real fact, to wit, that the body always accompanies our thought and exists with it.

319. Distinction between Psychological Phenomena and Physiological Phenomena. — We must then put aside, as without value, the Cartesian argument, and find elsewhere, if it is possible, the legitimate basis of spiritualistic beliefs.

Will the difference between psychological and physiological phenomena, on which we have no longer to dwell (see Chapter I.), suffice to attain this end ?

Assuredly these two orders of phenomena are profoundly distinct, the first immediately illumined by the consciousness, the other plunged in the night of the unconscious. But from the difference between the two series of phenomena is it legitimate to infer a distinction between the causes which produce them ? What reply shall be made to the materialists who will say to us : Doubtless consciousness is something different from the unconscious movement of the particles of matter, and from the physical vibrations of the cerebral molecules; but it is the consequence of them, and depends upon them. Do we not see every day, in the transformations of matter, a succession of very different phenomena, but nevertheless issuing from one and the same principle? Is not motion transformed into light and into heat? Why might not motion be transformed into thought?

320. Contradictory Attributes of Matter and Thought. — The sole conclusive reason which can be opposed to the materialist is that psychological phenomena and physiological phenomena are not only different, but contradictory. There is an absolute contradiction between the attributes of matter and the attributes of thought.

Matter being what we conceive that it is, a collection of divisible and innumerable molecules, it does not seem possible that it can be the principle of thought, whose simplicity or unity and also identity are revealed to us by the consciousness.

321. Unity of the Mind. — All the philosophers, from Plato and Aristotle to Kant and Condillac, have asserted the unity of thought. The intellectual operations consist in reducing plurality to unity.

To judge is to unite several ideas. To reason is to unite several judgments. The fact is undeniable; what conclusions can be drawn from it? Matter, being essentially divisible, composed of parts, cannot be, we are assured, the principle of thought, since the subject of thought is necessarily one and simple.

Condillac has stated this argument with force and precision. "The body," he says, "as far as it is a complex whole, cannot be the subject of thought. Shall we really divide thought into all the substances of which it is composed? In the first place, this will not be possible if it is but a perception, one and indivisible; and in the second place, we must still abandon this supposition if thought is formed of a certain number of perceptions. Let A, B, and C be three substances which enter into the composition of bodies and are distributed into three different perceptions. I ask where the comparison will be made. It will not be in A, since we cannot compare a perception which we have with one which we do not have. For the same reason it will be neither in B nor in C. We must then admit a point of reunion, a substance which is at the same time a simple and indivisible subject of these three perceptions, and consequently distinct from the body, — in a word, a soul." [1]

322. Identity of the Mind. — An argument of the same kind is the one which is drawn from *personal identity*. In reality, notwithstanding the perpetual mobility of our states of consciousness, it is to the Ego that we refer this whole succession of feelings and thoughts. The identity of the Ego is verified by the memory

---

[1] Condillac, *Connaissance humaine*, part i., ch. i.

which reveals it, and which at the same time could not be explained without it ; for memory evidently supposes the continuity of one and the same existence. On the other hand, responsibility no longer exists if we do not admit the identity of the moral subject. I am responsible to-day for what I did yesterday, and for what I did a year or two years ago, only because I am the same person.

Now, matter is ever changing and renewing itself in all its particles. An incessant change of molecules takes place between our body and external bodies. This is what the physiologists call the *vital vortex*.

"In living bodies," says Cuvier, "no molecule remains in place, — all are coming and going successively ; life is a continual vortex whose direction, however complicated it may be, remains constant, even as the kind of molecules which are carried along in it, but not the individual molecules themselves. On the contrary, the actual matter of the living body will presently be there no longer, but yet it is the depository of the force which will constrain the future matter to go in the same direction in which it goes."

323. The Soul is a Force. — Another argument of the spiritualists consists in contrasting the inertia of matter, incapable of self-movement, with the spontaneity of thought, capable of self-determination.

"Every material molecule," says Janet, "receives action and communicates it to another molecule, but

does not itself produce it. Every movement is the
sequel and the transformation of prior movements.
Matter is *inert*, that is, incapable of changing its state ;
when at rest, it remains at rest ; when in motion, it
remains in motion." [1]

How then can we confound with inert matter the
principle of human will and liberty?

324. Objections of the Materialists. — Whatever may
be the force of the arguments which we have just
stated, it must be acknowledged that they do not suffice
to convince the materialists, nor to fix the spiritualist
beliefs on a positive basis, sheltered from all objection.
In this question neither the reason for, nor the reason
against, can pretend to absolute certitude ; and perhaps
materialism is even better refuted by the weakness of
its own arguments than by the force of the arguments
against it.

325. General Objections. — The materialists, especially
in the ancient schools, have laid great stress on the influence which age, decrepitude, and sickness exercise on
the development of thought.

The moral faculties grow with the physical forces, and
also decline and become extinct with them ; illness
abates them ; and our mind is at the mercy of an attack
of fever.   How, then, not believe, it is said, in the identity of two forces which, in their development, follow a
parallel course, and which grow, weaken, and perish together ?

[1] P. Janet, *Traité élémentaire de philosophie*, i., p. 337.

All these objections are connected with the wide
theme of the influence of the physical on the spiritual.
Indeed, it cannot be denied that the intellectual functions are in great part dependent on our physical
states.   An enlightened spiritualism will in no wise
deny the correspondence between the physical and
the moral.

Bossuet said, " Man is one and the same organic
whole ;" but to the influence of the physical on the
moral, the spiritualists properly oppose a series of contrary facts, all of which tend to establish the influence
of the spiritual on the physical.   The imagination, the
passions, will, and force of character, react on health
and the physiological functions, and thus give proof of a
spiritual force distinct from the physical forces, since,
to a certain extent, it can subject them to its control.
From all this it may doubtless be inferred that body
and mind are intimately connected, and that between
them there are profound relations and a mutual depend-
ence ; but it would be going beyond the legitimate
consequences of these facts if we were to infer from
them that the moral faculties are derived from the physical faculties.   "All would proceed in the same way,"
says Marion, "if the body were but the companion and
instrument of the moral life in this world."

326. Relation between Brain and Thought. — The arguments of contemporary materialists hardly insist longer
on the general relations between the physical life and

the moral life; they bear almost exclusively on the intimate relations between brain and thought.

Here is the doctrine enunciated in all its clearness : "I think every scientist," says Charles Vogt,* "is bound to think that all the faculties which we comprise under the name of the properties of the soul are but functions of the cerebral substance ; and if I may borrow a familiar comparison, that these thoughts have almost the same relation with the brain that the bile has with the liver, or the urine with the kidneys."

Thought, then, is a function, and even, according to the brutal comparison of Charles Vogt, "a secretion of the brain."

In their attempts to justify this assertion, the materialists invoke the results of cerebral analysis. They remind us over and over again that the very existence of thought is conditioned on the existence of a brain ; and that the development, the degree of thought, corresponds precisely to certain states of the brain. It is true that on this point wide differences of opinion are expressed, and that the materialists have come to no understanding among themselves as to the cerebral qualities which are the basis of thought.

According to some, it is the *weight* of the brain ; according to others, it is the *volume;* according to still others, it is the *chemical constitution* of the brain, — "without phosphorus, no thought ;" or according to others still, the greater or less complexity of the *cere-*

bral circumvolutions.[1] Appeal has even been made to the *form* and the *temperature* of the cerebral matter.

327. Criticism of this Objection.—Assuredly no one thinks of denying that the brain is the organ or instrument of thought. Just as we do not see without eyes, so we cannot think without the brain; and just as we see imperfectly with eyes injured by disease or by some lesion, so we think clearly only with a sound brain, a brain whose constitution remains normal.

But we shall immediately perceive, by the large number of conditions and cerebral qualities which they invoke one after another, that the materialists themselves recognize that they have not succeeded in determining, with precision, the cerebral principle of thought. If they appeal sometimes to the chemical constitution of the brain, and at others to the weight, volume, and to the complexity of its circumvolutions, it is because, in fact, experience contradicts their absolute theories on every point. It is said, for example, that in order to be a great mind, one must have a brain which weighs more than fifteen hundred grammes; and yet the facts are often in contradiction with this assertion. The truth is that the analysis of the brain is still incomplete and obscure on more than one point, and that science has not yet illumined the mysterious functions of that organ so delicate and so complex.

Moreover, had the materialists succeeded in coming

[1] On this subject see the excellent book of Paul Janet, *Le Cerveau et la Pensée.*

to an agreement, and in determining with exactness the relations between the brain and thought, they would indeed have shown the correspondence between physiological phenomena and spiritual phenomena, and would have shown that the brain is one of the conditions of thought ; but they would not yet have proved that it is the only condition. They would have made it apparent that the intelligence and the sensibility cannot do without the brain, just as the musician and the artist cannot do without an instrument ; but they would not have demonstrated that the brain is the very cause and principle of thought. Let us admit, if so desired, that the spiritualists cannot argue in favor of the existence of the soul by any decisive, positive, and truly scientific argument ; but we must not fail to recollect, also, that the materialists have not at their disposal absolute and irrefutable proofs to justify their thesis.

328. Substitution of One Part of the Brain for Another. — Let us observe, moreover, that the analysis of the brain is not always as favorable as the partisans of materialism assert, to the doctrine which they maintain. The facts which they allege are often in contradiction with their theories.

" If the different intellectual operations cease," says Ravaisson,* " when the brain is destroyed or even seriously injured, nevertheless, provided life continues, they become re-established after a longer or shorter time.

This is one of the most important results of the experiments of Flourens.* According to these experiments, for the cerebral hemispheres, which are the widest expansion of the nervous system, there were substituted, after a little time, the striated bodies, the expansion immediately above the spinal marrow, whose normal function is to serve the instinctive operations.

" It has, then, not only been proved true that a small part of the brain may, in case of need, suffice for all its functions; but it has been proved true that for the whole brain there may be substituted, even in the higher functions which properly belong to it, the parts of the nervous system which, in their normal and habitual state, serve only the functions which are proximately inferior. This proves that it is not the organ which causes the function, as the materialists claim, but that it is the function or the action which, under certain physical conditions, subjects and appropriates the organ." [1]

329. What is Matter? — It follows from the examination of the arguments for materialism, that its partisans are very far from having demonstrated the truth of their theory. The question of the existence of the soul thus remains an open question which science does not forbid us to solve in accordance with our natural aspirations, our feeling, and the popular belief. Doubt-

[1] F. Ravaisson, *Rapport sur la philosophie du xix. siècle*, p. 189.

less we seem to be condemned not to know the nature of the principle of thought, and never to attain at least a scientific conception of this principle. But in our turn, taking the offensive against the materialists, may we not remind them that they themselves have no definite idea of matter? The brain, you say, is not merely the condition of thought, but it is its cause and substance! But what is the brain itself? How do we know it, if not through thought itself? Positively, what are the fibres and nervous cells, if not the representations of thought and of the conceptions of our mind? To those who say all is matter, we have the right to reply, with more logic and certitude, all is thought! And to those who say, What is mind? we reply, What is matter?

SUMMARY.

191. The question of the **EXISTENCE OF THE SOUL** does not fall within the domain of empirical psychology; it belongs to natural psychology or metaphysics.

192. At all times, two contradictory doctrines with reference to the nature of the thinking principle have been confronted with each other, — **SPIRITUALISM** and **MATERIALISM**.

193. A natural instinct leads us to admit the **DUALITY OF HUMAN NATURE** and the co-existence of **MIND** and **BODY**.

194. The arguments of the spiritualists are not wholly conclusive. **THE REASONING OF DESCARTES**, based on the distinction between the idea of thought and the idea of body, in no wise proves the real separation of mind and body.

195. PSYCHOLOGICAL PHENOMENA and **PHYSIO-LOGICAL PHENOMENA** are profoundly distinct; but it is impossible to infer a separation of causes from the difference in effects.

196. There is more force in the argument which consists in showing that the attributes of matter and the attributes of thought are **CONTRADICTORY**.

197. Matter is **DIVISIBLE** and **EXTENDED**; thought supposes a **SIMPLE** and **UNIQUE** principle.

198. Matter is **CHANGEABLE** and is ever **RENEWING** itself in a sort of vital vortex; the mind remains **IDENTICAL**

199. Matter is **INERT**; the mind acts **SPONTANE-OUSLY** and **FREELY**.

200. The arguments of the materialists by no means suffice to prove that the soul does not exist.

201. The correlation between physical states and the development of the mind only proves the **NECESSARY CO-EXISTENCE** of thought and matter.

202. The **BRAIN** is doubtless the **INSTRUMENT OF THOUGHT**, but nothing proves that it is the principle of thought.

203. The peculiar power of the thinking principle manifests itself in the fact that certain parts of the brain may be substituted, as organs of thought, for other parts when the latter have been destroyed.

204. The materialists who say they are not able to conceive mind are themselves incapable of **DEFINING MATTER** and of proving its existence.

INDEX

306 INDEX

Aristotle (384-322 B. C.). A Greek philosopher, a pupil of Plato, the preceptor of Alexander the Great, the founder of a school of philosophy at Athens called the *Lyceum*. His doctrine is known as the *peripatetic*, so called from his method of teaching, which took place while walking. His influence was great during the Middle Age when people swore only by Aristotle. His researches embraced all parts of science, and he carried into all his investigations the positive spirit and the method of observation and experiment. His *Ethics*, or treatise on morals, is the most valuable part of his works. Education is discussed in the *Politics*.

Arnobius (-326). A Christian theologian of the third century.

Attributes. Synonymous with qualities : the intelligence, the sensibility, and the will are the moral attributes of human nature. In a narrower sense, *attributes* is a metaphysical term and applicable exclusively to the Divine nature.

Augustine, Saint (354-430). Bishop of Hippo, one of the Fathers of the Church.

Automatism. The characteristic of beings that move mechanically, without intelligence and will.

Bain, Alexander (1818-). A contemporary Scottish philosopher. His principal works are, " The Senses and the Intelligence," " The Emotions and the Will," and " Education as a Science."

Barthélemy Saint-Hilaire (1805-). A French philosopher and statesman, and translator of the works of Aristotle.

Bayle, Pierre (1647-1706). A celebrated French writer, and author of the *Dictionnaire historique et critique*, which has chiefly made his reputation and which is still consulted with profit. His philosophical ideas tend to scepticism, and he has often been considered as the precursor of Voltaire.

Berkeley, George (1684-1753). Irish bishop and philosopher, celebrated for his idealism, which he has set forth in his " Dialogues." Attempted to found a college at Newport, R. I.

Berthelot, P. E. M. (1827-). A contemporary French scientist.

Bonald, L. G. A. (1754-1840). A French philosopher, a theoretical advocate of absolute monarchy in his book *Législation primitive*. It is he who defined man as *an intelligence served by organs*. His philosophy is spiritualist and Catholic.

Bossuet, J. B. (1627-1704). A great French writer and theologian, who has contributed to philosophy proper by his *Traité de la connaissance de Dieu et de soi-même*, composed for the education of the Dauphin.

Buridan, Jean (1315?-1358). A philosopher of the Middle Age, a defender of nominalism, who was much interested in the question of free-will. It was he who stated the hypothetical case of the ass pressed by the double need of drinking and eating, and not knowing what resolution to take. The *âne de Buridan* has remained proverbial.

Categories. A logical term denoting the different species of our ideas, as the categories of substance, of quality, etc. Aristotle distinguished ten categories.

Cells. A term in natural history, denoting anatomical elements which unite with fibres to form tissues.

Cerebral circumvolutions. The sinuous furrows presented by the upper surface of the brain.

Cheselden, William (1710-). An English surgeon, celebrated for his skill in removing cataracts from persons born blind.

Coleridge, Samuel Taylor (1772-1834). An English philosopher and poet.

Comte, Auguste (1798-1857). A French philosopher and mathematician, founder of the positivist school, of which Littré, after Auguste Comte, was the most illustrious representative.

Conceptualism. A philosophical doctrine of the Middle Age, made illustrious by Abelard, which consisted in holding, with reference to *nominalism* and *realism*, that general ideas, or concepts, had a real value, but that they represented only the relations of things.

Condillac, E. B. (1715-1780). A French philosopher and teacher. In 1757 he became preceptor of the infant Duke of Parma, and composed for this occasion a *Cours d'étude* in sixteen volumes. His most important philosophical works are his *Essai sur l'origine des connaissances humaines*, and his *Traité des sensations*. Condillac belonged to the sensualist school, and held that all our ideas are derived from the senses. His doctrine remained dominant in French philosophy till 1815.

Contingent. The contrary of the necessary, that which happens (from the Latin *contingere*) or which may not happen.

Cuvier, Baron (1769-1832). A French naturalist, author of a large number of works: *Leçons d'anatomie comparée, Discours sur les révolutions du globe, Recherches sur les animaux fossiles, Règne animal distribué d'après son organisation*.

Daltonism. A visual infirmity which prevents one from distinguishing colors, so called from Dalton, an English physician (1766–1844), who was afflicted with it and described it.

Danaides. The fifty daughters of Danaus, who, according to the mythological account, were condemned, in the infernal regions, to keep a leaky barrel full of water, for having murdered their husbands.

Democritus (470?–351? B.C.). The author of the atomic philosophy, and the precursor of Epicurus.

Descartes, René (1596–1650). The greatest of the French philosophers. It was he who founded modern philosophy by substituting for the principle of authority the method of free examination. His chief works are the *Discours de la Méthode* and the *Méditations métaphysiques.* His doctrine is an idealistic spiritualism. Descartes was also a mathematician and a scientist — in a word, a universal scholar.

Degradation. The progressive diminution of light, shade, and color, to indicate successive degrees of remoteness.

Determinism. A philosophical and scientific term. In nature, the well-founded belief in the necessary action of the causal relation; in psychology, the questionable belief in the irresistible power of motive in our voluntary determinations.

Diderot, Denis (1713–1784). A great French writer, who touched on all subjects, and who, in philosophy, hesitated between materialism and pantheism.

Edict of the Prætor. Roman law pronounced by the prætor, who was charged with the administration of justice.

Efficient (cause). A philosophical term signifying the cause which precedes the effect and actually produces it.

Egger (1813–   ). A French Hellenist, and professor in the Sorbonne.

Elective (affinities). A term in chemistry and physiology denoting the natural forces which unite bodies and organs ; used metaphorically, in a moral sense, to designate the affections which represent a choice, an *election.*

Entity. A term in scholastic philosophy ; that which constitutes the substance of a thing, and might exist apart from the thing itself.

Epicurus (342–270 B.C.). A Greek philosopher who revived the atomic theories of Democritus, the founder of a school of morals that made of pleasure the purpose of life and that was opposed to stoicism.

Fibres. Anatomical elements, distinguished as muscular fibres and nervous fibres.

Fielding, Henry (1707–1754). A celebrated English novelist, author of " Tom Jones," " Joseph Andrews," " Jonathan Wild," " Amelia."

Final (cause), as distinguished from *efficient cause ;* the cause which is the purpose, the end of our actions, the final destination of things.

Flourens, M. J. P. (1794–1867). A French physiologist. His principal works are *Fonctions du système nerveux*, and *De l'instinct et de l'intelligence des animaux.*

Fouillée. A contemporary French philosopher, the author of a large number of works : *La philosophie de Socrate, La philosophie de Platon.*

Franklin, Benjamin (1706–1790). An American moralist and statesman.

Garnier, Adolphe (1801–1864). A French philosopher of the sensualist school, professor in the Sorbonne, the author of a book too little known, *Traité des facultés de l'âme.*

Golconda. A city of Hindostan, formerly a famous *entrepôt* of diamonds and precious stones.

Grace. A theological term, inward assistance granted by Heaven for the accomplishment of good and the sanctification of the soul, granted to some and refused to others.

Hamilton, Sir William (1788–1856). A Scotch philosopher, author of " Lectures on Metaphysics and Logic " and " Discussions on Philosophy and Education."

Harpagon. The principal character in Molière's comedy, *L'Avare.*

Hartmann, von, Edward (1840–   ). A contemporary German philosopher, author of " The Philosophy of the Unconscious."

Helvetius, Claude Adrien (1715–1771). A French philosopher belonging to the materialistic school ; author of the book *De l'esprit.*

Hemispheres. A term in anatomy ; the two lateral halves of the brain and the cerebellum.

Hobbes, Thomas (1588–1679). An English philosopher and political writer, a materialist in philosophy, and a partisan of absolutism in politics. He wrote " Human Nature," " De Corpore Politico," " Leviathan."

Holbach, von, Paul Henri (1723-1789). One of the leaders of the French materialistic school of the eighteenth century; author of *Système de la nature.*

Hugo, Victor (1802-1885). The greatest French poet of the century; author of *Les Misérables.*

Idealism, in philosophy, the doctrine opposed to materialism, which admits no other reality than ideas; the doctrine of Berkeley; in general, and in the fine arts, the tendency to seek the ideal.

Irenæus, Saint (140-202). A Father of the Church.

Interior tribunal, *For intérieur,* the judgment of the conscience, as distinguished from the exterior tribunal, which is the authority of human justice.

Janet, Paul (1823-   ). A contemporary French philosopher who belongs to the spiritualist school, a professor in the Sorbonne, and the author of a large number of works which have contributed to the revival of philosophical studies in France: *Histoire de la science politique dans ses rapports avec la morale, La Famille, La Morale, Les Causes finales,* etc.

Jouffroy, Théodore Simon (1796-1842). A French philosopher of the spiritualist school, particularly interested in psychology and ethics. His principal works have been collected in two volumes, entitled: *Mélanges philosophiques* and *Nouveaux mélanges.*

Justin, Saint (114-168). A Christian apologist.

Kant, Immanuel (1724-1804). With Leibnitz, the greatest of German philosophers. His principal works are: "Criticism of Pure Reason," "Criticism of Practical Reason." Kant denies the possibility of metaphysics, but he re-establishes belief in God, in the soul, and in liberty, by presenting them as conditions of morals. The school which he founded is called the *critical,* or the *critical philosophy,* and is represented in France by Renouvier.

Lamartine, de, A. M. L. (1790-1869). A great French poet and political writer. The part played by Lamartine in the Republic of 1848 is well known. His principal works are: *Méditations, Harmonies poétiques et religieuses, Jocelyn.*

La Rochefoucauld, de, François (1613-1680). A French moralist, author of the celebrated *Maximes.*

La Romiguière, Pierre (1756-1837). A French philosopher, one of the first who reacted against the sensualist tendencies of the school of Condillac. His best work is entitled *Leçons de philosophie*.

Leibnitz, Godfrey William (1646-1716). A great German philosopher whose doctrines resemble those of Descartes, spiritualist and even idealist. His principal works are: *Nouveaux essais sur l'entendement humain*, a criticism of Locke's work; *Théodicée*.

Lemoine, Albert (1824-). A French philosopher of the spiritualist school, a sagacious and penetrating psychologist.

Locke, John (1632-1704). An English philosopher, one of the first to apply the method of observation and experiment. His doctrine, which resembles sensualism, was very popular in France in the eighteenth century, after having been criticised by Leibnitz in the seventeenth century. His two great works are: "The Human Understanding" and "Thoughts on Education."

Logic. The part of philosophy which studies the processes of reasoning, the means of arriving at truth and of shunning error; and which treats of scientific methods.

Malebranche, Nicolas (1638-1715). French moralist and metaphysician, priest of the Oratory, celebrated for his *Vision en Dieu*, whom Voltaire bantered in these lines:

> Lui qui voit tout en Dieu,
> N'y voit pas qu'il est fou.

His great work, *La Recherche de la Vérité*, contains on the causes of errors some parts that are still worth reading.

Manichæans. Followers of Manes, a Persian philosopher (240-274).

Metaphysics. A part of philosophy, differently defined according to the schools, but now considered the search for what is beyond experience.

Micromégas. A name invented by Voltaire to designate one of the characters of the philosophical romance bearing this name.

Mill, John Stuart (1806-1873). One of the greatest thinkers of modern England, author of "A System of Logic," "Essays on Political Economy," and "The Philosophy of Sir William Hamilton."

Milton, John (1608-1674). An English poet, author of "Paradise Lost," one of the greatest epic poems of modern literature.

Misanthrope. One who hates men. The title given by Molière to one of his comedies in verse.

Mnemotechnics. Whatever relates to the art of improving and strengthening the memory.

Moleschott, Jacob (1822–   ). A contemporary Dutch scholar.

Montesquieu, de, BARON (1689–1755). A celebrated French writer, the author of *L'esprit des lois*.

Müller, Friedrich Max (1823–   ). A contemporary scholar, of German descent, living in England, where he has written in English his celebrated " Lectures on Language."

Musset, de, Alfred (1810–1857). With Lamartine and Victor Hugo, one of the three great French poets of this century.

Naturalism. The system which attributes everything to nature; in the fine arts, the tendency to copy nature without any pursuit of the ideal.

Newton, Sir Isaac (1642–1727). An English mathematician, natural philosopher, and astronomer. It was he who discovered the laws of universal attraction and of the decomposition of light; and he shares with Leibnitz the honor of having discovered the infinitesimal calculus.

Nominalism. The scholastic system which asserted that general ideas are but names (*nomina*).

Noumen. A term invented by Kant to designate, in opposition to *phenomena*, the things conceived by thought.

Objective. A term in philosophy to designate whatever relates to the object, as distinguished from the *subjective*, which relates to the subject or the mind.

Onomatapœias. Imitative words which reproduce the sounds made by the things which they signify.

Pantheism. A philosophical doctrine which confounds the universe with God and deifies nature. The word was coined about the year 1700, by the English philosopher, John Toland. The principal philosophers of this school are, in antiquity, Parmenides and the Alexandrians, and, in modern times, Spinoza and Hegel.

Pascal, Blaise (1623–1662). A great French writer and moralist, the author of the *Provinciales* and *Pensées*, a mathematician and natural philosopher.

Pérez, Bernard. A contemporary French philosopher, who has especially devoted himself to the pursuit of pedagogical psychology, the author of a great number of works : *Les trois premières années de l'enfant*, *Education dès le berceau*, *L'Enfant de trois à sept ans*, etc.

Pellico, Silvio (1788–1854). An Italian poet, persecuted for his liberal and political opinions by the Austrian government. Author of *Le Mie Prigioni*.

Phrenology. The system of Gall and Lavater, which localizes the faculties in different parts of the brain.

Plato (427–347 B. C.). With Aristotle, the greatest of the Greek philosophers, the immediate pupil of Socrates, whose doctrines he has not always faithfully reproduced, being as much drawn towards idealism as Socrates was from it. His ethics, set forth in the *Gorgias* and in other dialogues, is admirable. His politics and his pedagogy, formulated in the *Republic* and the *Laws*, are in part chimerical.

Polyanimism. A primitive belief, which ascribes souls to all existences.

Polytheism. A primitive religion, which admits a great number of divinities.

Pope, Alexander (1688–1744). An English poet, author of the " Essay on Man."

Positivism. A philosophical system founded by Auguste Comte, which discards all theological or metaphysical doctrine, and bases itself exclusively on the positive sciences.

Predestination. A theological term signifying the purpose formed by God from all eternity to cast away certain men and to save others.

Premises. The major and the minor of a syllogism, the propositions on which is based the conclusion of the reasoning.

Rabelais, François (1483–1553). The celebrated author of *Gargantua and Pantagruel*, a satirical and burlesque romance in which, notwithstanding many uncouth fancies, there are presented some profound views on education.

Racine, Jean (1639–1699). A great French tragic poet.

Ravaisson, J. G. F. (1813–   ). A contemporary French philosopher, of idealistic tendencies, author of *La Philosophie l'Aristote*, *L'Habitude*, and *La Philosophie en France au xix. siècle*.

Realism. In philosophy, a doctrine of the Middle Age, which admits as many distinct substantial realities as there are general terms in language; in the fine arts, the tendency to ignore the ideal and to be content with an ex ct description of reality.

Receptivity. A didactic term, the faculty of receiving impressions.

Reid, Thomas (1710–1796). A Scottish philosopher, founder of the school known as the Scotch, which is especially noted for its psychological and practical tendencies, and for its repugnance for metaphysical researches.

Renan, Joseph Ernest (1823–   ). French orientalist, author and critic, author of *Vie de Jésus*, one of the most brilliant writers of the day.

Reyer. A contemporary German philosopher, author of a book recently translated into French, *L'Âme de l'enfant.*

Royer-Collard, Pierre Paul (1763–1845). A French philosopher and statesman.

Sand, Georges (1804–1876). The illustrious author of a large number of romances; the *nom de plume* of Madame A. L. A. Dudevant.

Schiller, von, J. C. F. (1759–1805). One of the greatest poets of Germany.

Scholasticism. The doctrines of the scholastics or schoolmen, the philosophy taught in the schools of the Middle Age, whose characteristic was subserviency to Catholic philosophy.

Sensualism. "The doctrine that all our knowledge is derived originally from the senses."

Simon, Jules (1814–   ). A French philosopher and statesman.

Socrates (470–400 B. C.). The founder of Greek philosophy.

Sophism. False reasoning which has some appearance of truth.

Spencer, Herbert (1829–   ). A contemporary English philosopher, one of the great thinkers of the age. His principal works are "Education" and "First Principles."

Spinoza, Baruch or **Benedict** (1632–1677). A celebrated Dutch philosopher, author of a work on ethics in which he has set forth in a geometrical form his fatalistic and pantheistic philosophy.

Spiritualism. "The doctrine that there are substances or beings which are not cognizable by the senses, and which do not reveal themselves to us by any of the qualities of matter. . . . Spiritualism, grounded upon consciousness, preserves equally God, the human person, and external nature, without confounding them and without isolating the one from the other."

Spontaneity. The characteristic of actions which are self-producing.

Stimulus. Whatever is of a nature to determine an excitation in animal nature and consequently in moral nature.

Stoics. A sect of philosophers which sprung up in Greece and Rome three centuries before the birth of Christ. The Stoics admitted no good but virtue, in opposition to the Epicureans, who placed happiness in pleasure. The principal moralists belonging to this school are Epictetus, Seneca, and Marcus Aurelius.

Subjective. That which relates to the subject, that which takes place in the interior of the mind, in opposition to the *objective*.

Substratum. A term in philosophy, that which serves as a support to qualities, that which exists independently of qualities, which lies beneath them.

Sully, James. A contemporary English psychologist, author of "Outlines of Pyschology" and "Teacher's Handbook of Psychology."

Swift, Jonathan (1667-1745). An English man of letters, author of "Gulliver's Travels."

Tertullian (160-245). A Father of the Christian Church.

Theresa, Saint (1515-1582). A celebrated mystic.

Thierry, Augustin (1795-1850). A celebrated French historian.

Tyndall, John (1820-   ). A contemporary English physicist.

Universals. A scholastic term, the categories of general ideas. Five universals were distinguished : genus, species, difference, property, and accident.

Vauvenargues (1715-1747). A French moralist, whose *Maximes* refute those of La Rochefoucauld.

Virgil (69-19 B. C.). The greatest of Latin poets, author of the *Bucolics*, the *Georgics*, and the *Æneid*.

Vogt, Charles (1817-   ). A German naturalist.

Wolf, Christian (1679-1745). German philosopher, a disciple of Leibnitz.

www.ingramcontent.com/pod-product-compliance
Lightning Source LLC
Chambersburg PA
CBHW021214270326
41929CB00010B/1124